Michel Foucault and the
Subversion of Intellect

Michel Foucault and the Subversion of Intellect

KARLIS RACEVSKIS

Cornell University Press

ITHACA AND LONDON

First published 1983 by Cornell University Press.
Published in the United Kingdom by Cornell University Press Ltd.,
Ely House, 37 Dover Street, London W1X 4HQ.

International Standard Book Number 0-8014-1572-1
Library of Congress Catalog Card Number 82-22090
Printed in the United States of America
Librarians: Library of Congress cataloging information appears
on the last page of the book.

The paper in this book is acid-free and meets the guidelines for permanence and durability of the Committee on Production Guidelines for Book Longevity of the Council
on Library Resources.

To André Perbal, my first mentor,
sometime *instituteur*, and longtime friend

and in memory of my mother, 1911–1981

Contents

Acknowledgments

While working on the subject of this book, I have benefited
from a number of fortunate circumstances and valuable op-
portunities. I began writing on Michel Foucault during the
course of a memorable NEH Summer Seminar directed by
Edward W. Said in 1978. I am thankful to Michael Sprinker,
Paul Bové, and Jonathan Arac for involving me in a conference and a workshop on Foucault. I am most grateful for a
fellowship from the Society for the Humanities at Cornell
University, through which I was able to accomplish the bulk
of my work in a thoroughly enjoyable scholarly atmosphere.
For the quality of that experience, I thank two of the society's
directors, Michael Kammen and Eric A. Blackall, and their
assistants, Anne-Marie García, Olga Vrana, and Pamela
Dubert. While at Cornell, I also profited from discussions
with Philip E. Lewis. My editors, Bernhard Kendler and Kay
Scheuer, have my gratitude for their support and the professional care with which they helped shape the final product.
Lastly, I would like to record my obligation to my family: my
children, my wife Maija, our parents, all of whom provided
a patient and understanding backing that I frequently took
for granted.

Parts of the last chapter have already appeared in print
and I thank the journals involved for permission to reprint
segments of the following articles: "The Theoretical Violence

Acknowledgments

of a Catastrophical Strategy," *Diacritics* 9, no. 3 (Fall 1979); "Un phénomène culturel récent: Adhésions et résistances à Michel Foucault," *The Proceedings of the Pacific Northwest Council on Foreign Languages*, Part 1, ed. John T. Brewer (Corvallis, Ore.: PNCFL, 1979); and "The Discourse of Michel Foucault: A Case of an Absent and Forgettable Subject," *Humanities in Society* 3, no. 1 (Winter 1980).

KARLIS RACEVSKIS
Dayton, Ohio

Works of Foucault
Cited in the Text

HF   *Folie et déraison: Histoire de la folie à l'âge classique.* Paris: Plon, 1961. Second edition: *Histoire de la folie à l'âge classique.* Paris: Gallimard, 1972.

MC   *Madness and Civilization: A History of Insanity in the Age of Reason.* Trans. Richard Howard. London: Tavistock, and New York: Pantheon, 1965. This is a considerably shortened version of the original.

BC   *The Birth of the Clinic: An Archaeology of Medical Perception.* Trans. Alan Sheridan. London: Tavistock, and New York: Pantheon, 1973. *Naissance de la clinique.* Paris: P.U.F., 1963.

OT   *The Order of Things: An Archaeology of the Human Sciences.* Trans. Alan Sheridan. London: Tavistock, and New York: Pantheon, 1970. *Les mots et les choses.* Paris: Gallimard, 1966.

AK   *The Archaeology of Knowledge.* Trans. Alan Sheridan. London: Tavistock, and New York: Pantheon, 1972. *L'archéologie du savoir.* Paris: Gallimard, 1969.

DL   *The Discourse on Language.* Trans. Rupert Swyer. Published as an appendix to the American edition of *The Archaeology of Knowledge. L'ordre du discours: Leçon inaugurale au Collège de France prononcée le 2 décembre 1970.* Paris: Gallimard, 1971.

DP   *Discipline and Punish: The Birth of the Prison.* Trans. Alan Sheridan. London: Allen Lane, 1977, and New York: Pantheon, 1978. *Surveiller et punir.* Paris: Gallimard, 1975.

HS   *The History of Sexuality.* Vol. 1: *An Introduction.* Trans. Robert Hurley. New York: Pantheon, 1978, and London: Allen Lane, 1979. *La volonté de savoir: Histoire de la sexualité,* vol. 1. Paris: Gallimard, 1976.

Works of Foucault

LCMP *Language, Counter-Memory, Practice: Selected Essays and Interviews.* Ed. with an introduction by Donald F. Bouchard and trans. Donald F. Bouchard and Sherry Simon. Ithaca: Cornell University Press, and Oxford: Blackwell, 1977.

PK *Power/Knowledge: Selected Interviews and Other Writings, 1972–1977.* Ed. with afterword by Colin Gordon and trans. Colin Gordon, Leo Marshall, John Mepham, Kate Soper. New York: Pantheon, 1980.

Fuller bibliographies of works by and on Michel Foucault can be found in Enrico Corradi, *Filosofia della "morta dell' uomo": Saggio sul pensiero di Michel Foucault* (Milan: Università Cattolica, 1977), in Alan Sheridan, *Michel Foucault: The Will to Truth* (London: Tavistock, and New York: Methuen, 1980), and in *Power/Knowledge* (cited above).

Michel Foucault and the
Subversion of Intellect

Introduction

It seems appropriate to begin a book on Michel Foucault with a number of disclaimers because the subject is in many ways an intimidating one. The breadth, depth, and scope of Foucault's analyses, the abstract configuration of his arguments, and the unsettling radicalness of his approach are all aspects that bring out the pretentiousness of any attempt at encapsulating his thought. Whence the necessity to point out, at the very beginning, that I have not tried to write a book about Michel Foucault in order to produce a survey or a systematic interpretation of "the man and his work." My principal aim has been to outline an intellectual strategy that I consider to have been profoundly liberating in its effects, to examine what I view as his successful attempt at dismantling the system of constraints with which Western civilization has established the norms and limits of humanity.[1] I have therefore sought to delineate the critical relation Foucault's discourse maintains with the intellectual traditions that have produced our civilization and its truths in order to

1. I find it noteworthy that Foucault has himself recently identified an intention "to create a history of the different modes by which, in our culture, the human being has been made a subject" as the main purpose behind his archaeological enterprise, at a speech made at the conference "Knowledge, Power, History," organized by the University of Southern California Center for the Humanities, October 31, 1981.

15

underscore the fundamentally subversive thrust of Foucault's archaeological and genealogical approaches.

This archaeology and genealogy thus constitute the subject of my work. Although it is not really possible to separate the two terms and although they are too vague to characterize the nature of Foucault's enterprise in more than a very general way, it is important to draw some distinctions between them. To put it simply, archaeology is the method with which a genealogical purpose can be realized. Archaeology provides the necessary tools for effecting a fundamental reversal in the ingrained habits of our intellectual existence and thus produces the approach necessary for constituting a "genealogy of the subject," for uncovering the mechanisms that have served all systematic attempts at understanding and defining man: the means are archaeological, the ends genealogical. Foucault's approach thus replaces the familiar opposition of form and content with discursive event/conditions of possibility and brings out areas of experience that have traditionally been covered up by an obsessive emphasis on the positive and the empirically verifiable. Instead of seeking to circumscribe meaningful discourses with the familiar devices of commentary or interpretation, Foucault wishes to reveal the historical conditions that make a particular mode of conceptualization possible and seeks to uncover the discursive and institutional strategies that contribute to the formation of subjects. It is the constitution of "objective" systems of knowledge that institutes subjection; by outlining the circumstances attending the formation of a discourse, Foucault reveals the basically political role of discourse in the formation of meanings—the meanings necessary for the constitution of man's images of himself.

If we consider the notion of discourse in its most general sense as the abstraction of any written or oral process of communication through which meaning is transmitted, as "the visible and describable praxis of what is called 'thinking,' "[2] then we have to grant, of course, that Foucault's own manner of dealing with discourse is—discursive. And when he recommends that "we must conceive discourse as a violence that we do to things, or, at all events, as a practice we impose upon them" (*DL*, p. 229), he is well aware that his own writing partakes of a certain violence and carries with it the power that inevitably accompanies epistemological inquisitions. But it is also the very awareness of this paradoxical situation that gives his strategy its subversive potential. For, while an archaeological methodology implies a particular epistemological predisposition, while a genealogical purpose connotes an ethical commitment, it is not the construction of systems that Foucault's discourse intends or achieves; rather, it is the systematic subversion of existing modes of explanation and rationalization. Foucault is therefore in sympathy with the aims of such disciplines as psychoanalysis, ethnology, and linguistics because the approaches to language or to conscious forms of representation these disciplines employ inevitably take into account the attending unconscious modes of discursive formation. These approaches see the subject not as a given, but as an entity linked to and dependent on various structures of consciousness. However, Foucault refuses to follow these disciplines specifically beyond the point at which they become disciplines, that is, organize themselves into methodologies purporting to find or to produce truth. He also refuses to follow those major figures of Western culture in whose names certain dogmatic systems have evolved, defining our truth and outlining our destiny, and although he obviously finds a number of Marxist and Freudian insights useful, Marx and Freud represent the sort of intellectual presence that Foucault intends to discredit.

Similarly, with regard to his own discourse, the seemingly systematic and systematizing conceptual models that he has

2. Timothy J. Reiss, *The Discourse of Modernism* (Ithaca: Cornell University Press, 1982), p. 9. For a fuller discussion of "discourse" see also Reiss, pp. 27–31 and *passim*.

_eveloped play an ambiguous role. They are used to dismantle existing modes of intellection, to reveal mechanisms that have kept us locked in specific, limited, and limiting formations of knowledge; they are not intended to serve as an epistemological alibi, as a "transcendent ineffable," or as the ontological elements necessary for the constitution and validation of a new rationality.[3] Foucault does not wish to erect new boundaries delimiting human nature; his discourse is not aimed at human beings but at other discourses. He therefore does not attempt to discredit individuals, does not blame social classes or groups: these are but subjects—that is, discursive constructs. In this regard, Foucault's approach to discourse can be considered similar to that of Jacques Lacan, for whom "a signifier is that which represents a subject . . . not for another subject, but for another signifier."[4] A signifier does not serve to link an individual to another individual or

3. The discourse of Foucault presents a challenge to its readers and critics by refusing to reveal what David Couzens Hoy has called the "transcendent ineffable," that is, either an epistemological, ontological, ethical, or aesthetic assumption, which constitutes the motivating force behind the discourse. Certain critics believe such a motivation to be inherent in some of the peculiarly Foucaldian terms and concepts, notions that suggest Foucault's adherence to the "traditional ideal of a self-legitimating discourse" and explain his inability to escape a familiar aporia. See Hoy's "Taking History Seriously: Foucault, Gadamer, Habermas," _Union Seminary Quarterly Review_ 34 (Winter 1979), 85–95; see also David Carroll, "The Subject of Archeology or the Sovereignty of the Episteme," _MLN_ 93 (1978), 695–722. The most systematic attempt to explain Foucault in terms that derive from his particular practice of discourse is to be found in the work of Hayden White. See, for example, "Foucault Decoded: Notes from Underground," which first appeared in _History and Theory_ 12, no. 1 (1973), and has been republished in _Tropics of Discourse: Essays in Cultural Criticism_ (Baltimore: The Johns Hopkins University Press, 1978); see also "Michel Foucault," in _Structuralism and Since: From Lévi-Strauss to Derrida_, ed. John Sturrock (Oxford: Oxford University Press, 1979). The critical thrust of White's essays appears to stem from his postulate of a Foucaldian consciousness, a catachrestic function in terms of which the text is to be decoded. Accordingly, White's project of decoding Foucault entails an explanatory strategy that derives its persuasiveness from a codification, oriented by a tropological perspective, that White imposes on Foucault's writings.

4. Jacques Lacan, _Le séminaire, Livre XI_ (Paris: Seuil, 1973), pp. 180–81.

to the world but to other signifiers; the subject is therefore an effect of the realm of signifiers and the subject's reality is provided by a field of discourses. To put it in Lacanian terms, the experience of the Real is made possible by the simultaneous mediation of two correlative functions—the Symbolic and the Imaginary.

The similarity between Foucault's treatment of discourse and a certain anthropological and psychoanalytical approach to the question of the subject constitutes the main heuristic motivation for my project; it is also the justification of this attempt to read Foucault in the light of the tripartite configuration of the Symbolic, the Imaginary, and the Real. To this, I must quickly add that I have not applied "Lacan" in some systematic fashion to Foucault's discourse. But I have found some Lacanian concepts as well as insights developed by Marcel Mauss and Claude Lévi-Strauss very helpful in understanding Foucault's critical strategy—a strategy that continually reasserts its connections to the paradoxical situation of the subject.

My critical examination of Foucault's archaeology begins, then, with an inquiry into the problematic of the subject and a discussion of the particular approach I use. If there is one thing that reading Foucault produces, it is, quite understandably, an increased sense of self-consciousness. Thus the act of writing about Foucault appears to be not only pretentious, as I have already suggested, but also subject to an inevitable contradiction: it imposes a closure on a discourse that has been most adept at discerning various strategies of epistemological closure. This act is therefore a responsibility one has to assume even while one mitigates the consequences of the act of interpretation by maintaining a vigilant awareness of one's tactics and trying to offset the inevitable areas of blindness with an emphasis on insights. The insight I wish to stress is meant to reveal Foucault's critical project as an effective instrument of change. To be sure, this leads me to impose an unwarranted unity on Foucault's oeuvre and to indulge in untested generalizations about "Western" civilization, man, discursive practices. My subject, however, is such that this tactic seems unavoidable. Thus, as I produce a particular image of Foucault's thought, I can only hope to maintain an adequate tension between the Imaginary and the Symbolic effects at work in this act of reading and writing.

In the final analysis, however, such an attempt to postpone identity indefinitely by refusing to adopt a concrete position is not simply dictated by some notion of intellectual integrity. It is related to a basic aspect of Foucault's critical purpose: the self-consciousness that we derive from Foucault's text is a fundamentally critical tool with which to locate ourselves as subjects in and of our own discursive practices. One of the principal insights provided by Foucault's writings is an understanding of the intricate and deceitful ways in which discourse establishes knowledge and imposes truths. This insight pertains to the question of our identity, but even more to the eminently political nature of discourses; it points to Foucault's involvement with particular kinds of struggles, those which, as he puts it, "revolve around the question 'who are we?' They are a refusal of the abstraction of economic and ideological State violence which ignores who we are collectively or individually, and also a refusal of scientific and administrative inquisition which determines who you are."[5] This resistance to the imposition of meaning comes from the realization that, although truth appears disinterested, it is not: it works to further very specific economic and political interests.

This duplicity of truth is in turn attributable to the manner in which power-knowledge strategies operate in society. Seen as a systematic attempt to impose a rational grid on a collectivity of human existences, society is an inherently flawed and highly deficient process, intended as it is to ad-

5. Foucault, speech at USC.

minister much of what is beyond the reach of rational understanding and control. This fundamental inadequacy is covered up, however, by institutions and official representations of social reality, by discourses whose purpose is to explain the problems the very existence of society has caused. As a result, certain standards of righteousness and norms of behavior are set up, and it becomes possible not only to delimit but to justify domains of exclusion, areas for containing all the misfits, all the enemies, those whose very existence in society would serve to demonstrate its healthy state. It is possible then to distinguish two strategies: one purposeful, interested in proclaiming the truth and in defending the status quo; the other anonymous, operating beyond the realm of conscious and rational control but effective in setting up areas of exclusion as well as of privilege, areas which eventually gain official recognition through the alibi of a subsequent rationalization.

Although Foucault notes thus an inevitable "relationship between rationalization and excesses of political power,"[6] he does not advocate the rejection of reason. An appeal to unreason is considered equally futile, simply because unreason is not the opposite of reason: it serves to support the latter. What is needed is an understanding of the conjunction that unites unreason to reason, death to life, the Other to the Same, the Symbolic to the Imaginary. The key to this understanding is language. Consequently, the investigation of the reality of discourse represents a crucial first stage in Foucault's critical enterprise. It is this investigation, I wish to argue, which has made the radicalness of Foucault's critique possible and which effectively sets his archaeological approach in opposition to traditional modes of intellection.

My own strategy will be to discuss Foucault's writing in order to highlight its capacity for reorienting our thinking with regard to the function, the effect, and the uses of dis-

6. Ibid.

course. Following an introductory chapter in which I outline the problematic of the subject, I examine Foucault's books on madness and on the clinic. Although the archaeological project is still vague in *Madness and Civilization* and in *The Birth of the Clinic*, it is already possible to distinguish the peculiar thrust of Foucault's investigations: they are directed not at some reality called mental or physical illness but at the coherence of a perception that posits a certain reality. Thus he shows that once such a reality is established, it becomes possible to organize systems of discursive practice known as sciences—legitimate and legitimizing fields of knowledge entrusted with overseeing and ordering human existence according to the epistemological schemes they develop.

These cognitive systems are not completely free to develop their schemes, however. They are subject to the rule of an *episteme*—an invisible pattern that serves as a fundamental regulatory mechanism for the formation of knowledge. The notion of the *episteme* is central to *The Order of Things* and is the subject of my third chapter. The fourth chapter deals principally with *The Archaeology of Knowledge* and examines Foucault's attempt at outlining the highly abstract design of his archaeological enterprise. I find the notion of the *énoncé* to be crucial here, as it points both to the factuality and the factitiousness of all discursive activity. It represents the undeniable yet inaccessible material reality of the statement and is instrumental in effecting the strategic reversal that characterizes an archaeological approach to discourse.

Archaeology's tactic of inversion is examined in Chapter 5. While inversion is a convenient term to use, it is not intended to suggest a simple reversal or a dialectic. Archaeology's principal merit, I believe, is to have undertaken the analysis of discourse in a radically new mode and to have placed it in the context of what Foucault calls a field or a space of dispersion: discourse is no longer seen in terms of a unifying referent, a content or a form; it is understood from the perspective of the connections it maintains with a network of discursive and nondiscursive activities. This new perspective, in turn, allows Foucault to link discourses to the everyday existence of men and women and to show that, since the functioning of discourse is inevitably political, the constitution of knowledge is inseparable from the exercise of power. In Chapters 6 and 7 I use *Discipline and Punish* and *The History of Sexuality*, as well as a number of Foucault's essays to outline the archaeological insights and practical applications illustrated by these works.

Foucault's attempt to undermine the rule of knowledge, to discredit the hegemony of reason, to reveal scientific discourse as a model that repeats itself analogically, that claims objectivity but is suffused with ideology—these are clearly endeavors that point to a special, perhaps radically new conception of the role of intellect. In my last three chapters I consider the effectiveness and usefulness of Foucault's approach, the dilemmas it raises, and the implications his critical stance holds for intellectual activism in general. I find it helpful to compare archaeology with other, more traditional approaches and, by way of defining and delimiting more precisely the area of Foucault's critique, I conclude my book with a brief survey of some of the positions espoused by admirers and detractors. Such a comparative study is also revealing for its capacity to highlight both a separation and an unbreakable connection between Foucault's discourse and its cultural context.

This ambiguous relationship is most striking when we juxtapose Foucault's work to that of his most notorious critic, Jean Baudrillard. The concern with techniques of control and normalization, with codes produced by a political economy, the understanding of cultural systems in terms of binary opposites working to conceal self-serving interests, the inversion of traditional explanatory sequences to show that truth is always a derivative of a process that precedes it— these are all themes that point to a striking similarity of purposes. At the same time, Baudrillard's critique is potentially the most damaging because it accuses archaeology of entering into collusion with precisely what the latter claims to combat, that is, with the existing hegemony of logic and reason. I find this confrontation useful because it sheds a new light on Foucault's writings. Furthermore, it lets us perceive the position of Baudrillard as an extreme that Foucault's archaeology has been careful to avoid. In the context of what has been called "the French Nietzscheanism of the last twenty years," it is Baudrillard who appears to have adopted a truly nihilistic stance.[7] Foucault has sought to develop the more affirmative thrust of Nietzschean insights by endeavoring to illustrate the endless consequences of the realization that "rational thought is interpretation according to a scheme which we cannot escape."[8] In contrast to the pretentiousness of those critical discourses that claim both to demystify and to surpass this scheme—those discourses that pretend in the original sense of *praetendere*, stretching and spreading out over the contemporary cultural scene in the manner of a curtain, or perhaps a shroud—the discourse of Michel Foucault realizes its critical effectiveness by maintaining a contiguous, metonymical relation with the intellectual matrix to which, after all, it owes its subversive potential.

7. Vincent Descombes, *Modern French Philosophy* (Cambridge: Cambridge University Press, 1980), p. 188.

8. "Notes" (1887), in Walter Kaufmann, ed. and trans., *The Portable Nietzsche* (New York: Viking, 1968), p. 455.

1

The Paradox of the Subject

Does man really exist? Posing this question in *The Order of Things* brought Michel Foucault a notoriety that soon propelled him to the foreground of the Parisian intellectual scene. Seen from the perspective of a Western humanistic discourse, the question does indeed seem to embody an outrageous paradox. For Foucault, however, it is a profoundly meaningful and earnest inquiry, one that raises the fundamental issue of the existence of Western man—one that focuses on the appearance of Western man as a subject, as the subject *in* and *of* his own discourse. To be sure, a subject that can both speak and be spoken of does not constitute a paradox attributable to Foucault, or anyone else. It is inherent in the ordinary usage of the term, be it French or English. The word in question has an inevitable ambiguity, since the "subject" of a discourse can be that which denotes as well as that which is denoted, it can both construct and be construed. According to *Webster's Third New International Dictionary*, a subject can be understood as the embodiment of thought, as something that sustains sense, but it can also be seen as something that has been brought under the authority, dominion, control, or influence of something that, in effect, has the capacity to "subject." Foucault's notable achievement is to show that these two aspects do not constitute a contradiction at all, that, taken as the foundation of discourse, the subject is a support on which discourse is erected but that it is, at the same time, dominated and controlled by the same discourse: it is both an active agent and an object acted upon. The subject is also an object—it is a product of discourse.

Raising the issue of man's being thus unavoidably brings up the problem of discourse—of what provides the subject with a reality and with a meaning. The difficulty concerns the curiously antagonistic coexistence of subject and discourse: the importance the subject gains through discourse has the effect of occulting the very source of the subject's ontological status, the discursive power to name. Foucault construes the subject as an obstacle to the development of a philosophical mode of thought that could adequately take into account mechanisms of signification and the formation of systems of meaning. The history of philosophical thinking has been dominated by what he calls the "philosophy of subject," which he defines as "a philosophy which sees the foundation of all knowledge and the principle of all signification as stemming from the meaningful subject."[1] Accordingly, one of Foucault's most evident aims—one of his avowed purposes—has been to dismantle the "transcendence of the ego" that he has found in the discursive practice of Western culture. This aim also manifests itself as a strategy intended to reveal the specific discursive mechanisms that have been effective in maintaining the subject in its paradoxical position of that which tells and is told.

The status of the subject has traditionally been guaranteed by what Foucault perceives as the characteristically anthropological configuration of Western discourse, a pattern whose development can be traced back to an epistemological break that takes place toward the beginning of the nineteenth century, when "man appears in his ambiguous position as an object of knowledge and as a subject that knows" (*OT*,

1. Foucault, "Truth and Subjectivity," Howison Lecture, delivered at the University of California at Berkeley, October 20, 1980.

p. 312). Man's knowledge of himself is determined by a basically circular process: it is constituted by his empirical experience of his existence; this experience, in turn, is broken down into the facts that both make up the framework of his thinking about himself and provide an epistemological validation for his systems of knowledge. Such a mode of intellection is inevitably anthropocentric, since "it is probably impossible to give empirical contents transcendental value, or to displace them in the direction of a constituent subjectivity, without giving rise, at least silently, to an anthropology—that is, to a mode of thought in which the rightful limitations of acquired knowledge (and consequently of all empirical knowledge) are at the same time the concrete forms of existence, precisely as they are given in that same empirical knowledge" (OT, p. 248). But the crucial issue for Michel Foucault is not simply an epistemological one: the anthropological bias is understood to provide knowledge with an insidious potential—with a propensity for turning into a political instrument of subjection.

An anthropological mode's strategic effectiveness at imposing its intellectual domination is due specifically to its built-in capacity for providing itself with an ethical and philosophical validation; it is attributable to its unquestioned privilege of defining the meaning, and thus, in effect, the being of man. Man's appearance in the field of discourse is seen by Foucault as the determining cause of a new mode of social existence: man has been subjected and reified as an object of knowledge, he has become a "body" in a field of forces, of power-knowledge strategies intent on effectively integrating the individual within the social scheme. These systems of power, Foucault shows, are products of knowledge; and power, in turn, helps constitute fields of investigation where truths are to be found. Furthermore, although power has manifested itself visibly in Western societies, · has been applied openly, without masks or covers, the circularity of power-knowledge mechanisms has remained the profound secret of their insidious efficacity. It is, for example, no coincidence that along with the new methods of classification, hierarchization, and codification, with the new techniques of subjection and coercion that developed at the beginning of the nineteenth century, the social sciences appeared. Since the early nineteen hundreds, the so-called human sciences have had as their specialty the "unglorious task" of making each individual they examine into a "case," that is, into "a case which at one and the same time constitutes an object for a branch of knowledge and a hold for a branch of power" (*DP*, p. 191). The development of Western discursive practice, especially in its official and institutionalized forms, has therefore favored the sort of discourse that actualizes domination and carries the potential for violence within its systematicness. At the basis of this discourse, Foucault discerns a will to knowledge or a will to truth that characterizes the manner in which discourse exerts its authority and establishes its limitations and exclusions. Such an impulsive desire to attain the ideal of a perfect understanding derives its force from the specific philosophical themes that justify a discursive purpose, themes that propose "an ideal truth as a law of discourse, and an immanent rationality as the principle of their behaviour. They accompany, too, an ethic of knowledge, promising truth only to the desire for truth itself and the power to think it." Yet the operation of these philosophical motifs is devious, because "they then go on to reinforce this activity by denying the specific reality of discourse in general" (*DL*, p. 227). The effectiveness of a discourse is thus attributed to its seemingly transparent and inconsequential mode of existence.

Foucault supposes that this particular reality of discourse has remained hidden from public view because of a profound logophobia that manifests itself in our culture as an instinctive turning away from the mysterious richness, disorder, and possible violence of discourse. The refusal to question the being of discourse has allowed for its "naturalization," has made it appear to be a natural emanation of thought, a purposeful expression of a subjective plenitude. And Foucault finds that it is precisely this "theme of the founding subject" which "permits us to elide the reality of discourse" (*DL*, p. 227). The theme of the subject is thereby linked to that of the anthropological artifice, and Foucault has concluded that any radical reflection on the reality of discourse and of language is not possible while discourse is the locus of a reflection on the being of man. Hence the need to undermine the Cartesian *Cogito*, which has been the constituting force underlying the experience of subjectivity. In order to conduct an effective investigation of the role discourse plays in our civilization, it becomes necessary to "throw off the last anthropological constraints," thanks to which Western discourse is still able to establish a cultural hegemony, exert its dogmatism, and preserve, "against all decenterings, the sovereignty of the subject, and the twin figures of anthropology and humanism" (*AK*, pp. 12 & 15).

In pursuing his project of demystification, Foucault has expressed a feeling of solidarity with all those who before him "attempted to remould this will to truth and to turn it against truth at the very point where truth undertakes to justify the taboo, and to define madness; all those from Nietzsche, to Artaud and Bataille, [who] must now stand as (probably haughty) signposts for all our future work" (*DL*, p. 220). These antecedents, in a sense, constitute the ethical foundation for Foucault's undertaking, but his writing also evidences affinities with certain epistemological paradigms. Foucault himself recognizes that his enterprise meshes with an intellectual strategy that he finds to be a pervasive trend in contemporary culture: "The exploratory thrust [*la percée*] toward a language from which the subject is excluded, the bringing to light of a perhaps irremediable incompatibility between the apparition of language in its being and the consciousness of the self in its identity, is an experience that today is taking place in many cultural areas: in the simple act of writing as in the attempts to formalize language, in the study of myths and in psychoanalysis, also in the search for this Logos which constitutes, as it were, the place of all Western rationality."[2] Consequently, we can discern two movements in Foucault's approach to the question of discourse. The first apparent purpose is to dissolve the subject, to dismantle the founding notion of a subjective consciousness; then, in the void thus created at the center of discourse, it becomes possible to develop a new kind of awareness that will radically alter our thinking about discourse. It is the absence of the subject or the subject as nonbeing that allows for a new approach, yet paradoxically the question of the subject remains—for the subject is still a presence in discourse, although it is the presence of an absence. Indeed, the dissolution of a conscious subject does not eliminate the subject but produces a shift in perspective: we have oriented thought toward the unconscious subject. From an awareness of the Same we have moved to that of the Other. We have arrived at the dimension of the Symbolic.

It is indeed the level of the Symbolic that causes the subject to disintegrate while maintaining it as the *topos* of the Symbolic. The paradoxical situation of the subject, as we find it in the work of Foucault, can be grasped only if we locate it with respect to the Symbolic dimension—the dimension that makes signification possible, that provides the limit and the unifying totality of a signifying practice. Man is a being possessing the capacity to maintain a self-conscious perception of his existence, to form an identity that he believes originates within him. This truth, however, is a meaning that is already there, before him, and "all these contents that his knowledge reveals to him as exterior to himself, and older than his own birth, anticipate him, overhang him with all their solidity, and traverse him as though he were merely an object of nature, a face doomed to be

2. Foucault, "La pensée du dehors," *Critique* 229 (June 1966), 525.

erased in the course of history" (*OT*, p. 313). It is the Symbolic dimension opened up by language that allows a subject to be constituted, yet keeps him from ever uniting his identity with his being.

The notion of the Symbolic derives principally from the work of anthropologists carried out in the early twentieth century. The most important source is a treatise by the French anthropologist Marcel Mauss entitled *Essai sur le don: Forme et raison de l'échange dans les sociétés archaïques*.[3] In that work, Mauss describes forms of exchange in primitive societies as possessing at once religious, legal, moral, economic, aesthetic, morphological, and mythological meaning and shows that objects of exchange symbolize the communion and allegiance established among the members of archaic societies. The Symbolic effect of an exchange in which nothing is gained or lost also serves to reconcile man with his universe, to provide an intangible, yet necessary link with the mysterious totality that surrounds him. The Symbolic dimension introduces otherness, the presence of an absence, a third, mediating term that provides the element of cohesion essential for the formation of any cultural system. In his introduction to a selection of essays by Mauss, Claude Lévi-Strauss provides us with the following definition of culture: "Any culture can be considered an ensemble of symbolic systems first among which we may rank language, matrimonial rules, economic relations, art, science, religion. All these systems aim to express certain aspects of physical and of social reality, and even more, the relations these two types of reality enjoy one with the other and the relations that the symbolic systems enjoy among themselves."[4] A fundamental characteristic of all these systems is their incommensurability; each one of

3. The essay was published in 1925 and has been translated as *The Gift: Forms and Functions of Exchange in Archaic Societies* (Glencoe, Ill.,: Free Press, 1954).

4. Lévi-Strauss, "Introduction à l'œuvre de Marcel Mauss," in Marcel Mauss, *Sociologie et anthropologie* (Paris: Presses Universitaires de France, 1950), p. xix.

them is irreducible to any other level. Nevertheless, they co-exist and form a network of tacitly accepted correspondences that are made possible by the Symbolic nature of human thought. It is in this network that the subject finds the justification and the explanation for his existence. The Symbolic is the undeniable yet intangible reality of the subject, and any attempt to describe this reality springs from the futile hope of circumscribing "a particular domain which would be that of the ineffable, since it is language in its totality which is this original suspension of all given reality thanks to which all presence becomes expressible: the basis of human reality is precisely what makes it appear to be without basis."[5] Whence the ambiguous situation of the subject represented both as a consciousness and an unconscious, as an entity that seeks to establish its particular identity while deriving its meaning from the discourse of an ever-present collectivity.

The investigation of the Symbolic existence of the subject belongs to the domain of psychoanalytic theory, and it is unquestionably the work of Jacques Lacan that has made the most significant contribution to our understanding of the Symbolic and of the subject's integration into discourse.[6] Lacan's work is in this sense contiguous with Foucault's. For Lacan, as for Foucault, the question of the subject is fundamental to the whole problematic of man's relation to his world. It is a relation made possible by the Symbolic; accordingly, we owe our existence as subjects to the Symbolic experience: "The essential part of human experience," notes Lacan, "that which can properly be called the experience of the subject, the one to which is due the existence of the

5. Edmond Ortigues, *Le discours et le symbole* (Paris: Aubier-Montaigne, 1962), p. 227.

6. It is in Lacan's well-known *Discours de Rome* (1953) that we find the first full discussion of the Symbolic. This discourse, translated, thoroughly annotated, and perceptively commented upon by Anthony Wilden, appears in Lacan, *The Language of the Self* (Baltimore: The Johns Hopkins University Press, 1968).

subject, can be located at the level where the symbol arises."[7] It is the Symbolic capacity of the human mind that allows man to have a hold on reality, yet subjects are never in a position to establish control over the Real, since they are no more than relays or supports that insert themselves between the dimensions of the Real and of the Symbolic. Thus, man finds himself possessed by the Symbolic from the very first and at every moment of his existence. He does not produce his own meaning—this signification is already given to him: "This signification is a function of a certain language [*parole*], which is and isn't the language of the subject—he receives this language ready-made, he is a relay for it."[8] At the same time, however, it is by being implicated in the process of language that the subject gains an identity—an individual reality that he acquires in the order of the Imaginary.

According to Lacan, there are two modes in which the subject apprehends reality: the Symbolic and the Imaginary. Since they are thoroughly interdependent, the subject is to be located at the intersection of the three axes of the Real, the Imaginary, and the Symbolic. The Symbolic order, as we have seen, constitutes the subject's meaning, determines his place in the world among other subjects, and allows him to form an identity by overseeing his entry into the order of the Imaginary. The Imaginary, in turn, is the order in which the subject develops a consciousness centered on itself. The constitution of a consciousness in an Imaginary dimension occurs at an early stage of infancy, during a period that Lacan calls the mirror-phase, when the child acquires an identity by seeing himself reflected in the perception of others: the others form a mirror that reflects the individual's being and produces his Self. And although it is the Symbolic that over-

7. Jacques Lacan, *Le séminaire, Livre II* (Paris: Seuil, 1978), pp. 255–56.
8. Ibid., p. 374. The word *parole* can have various connotations in the work of Lacan including those of Word, Logos, of language in the sense of "code," or of "utterance." For a discussion of the problems relating to the translation of Lacan, see Wilden in *The Language of the Self*, pp. xiv–xix and 91–156.

sees the world of our perception, it is the Imaginary that represents the fundamental and central structure of our experience.[9] However, the Imaginary mode of apprehending existence is fundamentally deceitful, since it owes its powers of conviction to a conceit that tends to occult the Symbolic dimension. The Imaginary leads us to think that we are in direct touch with reality, that we are in full possession of our knowledge, and that we can grasp the truth of our Selves. This truth is no more than a lure, of course, since we find it in a mirror: the identity that we gain in the Imaginary is given to us by others, it is an objectification centered upon the evidence of a conscious that is inevitably subject to a network of determinants already in place. The Self is thus a mirage and its relation to the world in which it sees itself reflected is constantly undermined by uncertainty. Thus, the certitude granted by the Cartesian *cogito* is actually profoundly alienating, since the objectifications the Self constructs simultaneously dispossess it of the truth it seeks.

It is to Freud's "Copernican revolution," Lacan tells us, that we owe this radically new understanding of a subject, whose reality is no longer self-centered but transindividual. It is this new awareness that allows us to see the being of the subject grounded in the inaccessible, the ineffable—in the unconscious, which is the discourse of the Other, the discourse of the circuit in which the subject finds himself integrated.[10] The unconscious is a product of language, it is produced by the power of the Word, and it constitutes the subject but withholds the subject's truth from him:

> The unconscious is the sum of the effects of language [*la parole*] on a subject, at the level where the subject is constituted by the effects of the signifier. This is to say that, with the term "subject," we do not designate the living substratum necessary for

9. Lacan delivered the original paper on the *stade du miroir* in 1936. A later version is to be found in his *Ecrits* (Paris: Seuil, 1966), pp. 39–109.
10. Lacan, *Séminaire II*, p. 11 and *passim*.

the subjective phenomenon, nor any other kind of substance, nor any being of knowledge in its primary or secondary affectivity [*pathie*], nor even the *logos* which supposedly is incarnated somewhere, but the Cartesian subject, which appears the moment when doubt recognizes itself as certitude—with this difference, that from our perspective, the foundations of this subject are seen to be much broader, but at the same time much more subservient, with regard to the certitude which escapes him.[11]

The Lacanian subject no longer finds his truth in a *cogito* because he sees himself dispersed by a field of signifiers that found his certitude but also make it dependent on a dimension that escapes him. To put it simply, Lacan transposes the Cartesian subject from the Imaginary to the Symbolic, from the realm of conscious certitude to that of intersubjective relations. In the Imaginary mode, language is seen to provide a direct contact between subjects or between a subject and reality; discourse, in this sense, is dissolved and replaced by the presence of objects produced by a coalescence of signifiers and their respective signifieds. For Lacan, the relation between signifier and signified is determined by the entire system of signifiers, it is a function of the order of language itself. There exists a gap, then, between a signifier and a signified, a disjunction that is covered up by a pact, by an acquiescence to language and its power to name: "Naming constitutes a pact by which two subjects simultaneously agree to recognize the same object. If human subjects refuse to name . . . , if subjects do not accept this recognition, there is no longer any world, even a world of perception, that could be sustained for even an instant. Here is the juncture, the appearance of the Symbolic with relation to the Imaginary."[12] By situating the subject at the intersection of the Symbolic with the Imaginary, Lacan underlines the basic ambivalence of language—which can be both a barrier

11. Lacan, *La séminaire, Livre XI* (Paris: Seuil, 1973), p. 116.
12. *Séminaire II*, p. 202.

and a link between subjects. This is so because "a signifier is that which represents a subject . . . not for another subject, but for another signifier."[13] The subject is therefore doubly determined by the law of language and by the effect of signifiers operative in the Symbolic: first, he finds himself in a field of relations that has already been set up by a network of signifiers; and second, his reality in an intersubjective context is liable to constant modifications because it is given by an order that escapes his control.

Praxis, from a Lacanian perspective, thus acquires a characteristically dual nature. Typical human behavior consists of apprehending the Real through the Symbolic while suppressing an awareness of the latter, and of producing Imaginary constructs that organize a world centered on the subject. Now, on the one hand, "the symbolic order [is] absolutely irreducible to what is commonly known as human experience."[14] On the other, because the two orders are absolutely dependent on each other, the production of meaning in the Imaginary would not take place without the creativity permitted by the Symbolic dimension. Similarly, the creative potential inherent in the Symbolic order would never materialize without the possibility offered by the Imaginary, which permits the crystallization of meaning and provides the grounding in reality necessary for any action. Seen as an oscillation between the Imaginary and the Symbolic, praxis may obviously evince a particular tendency toward one or the other of the two orders of perception. While the Imaginary provides for a systematic and purposeful ordering of our life-experience and permits objectification and differentiation, the Symbolic dimension both reveals and bridges the gap that separates our consciousness from the world. Perception dominated by the Imaginary mode tends to be rigid, finite, and fixed in precise patterns that form stereotypes of thought. Thus Anthony Wilden has noted that "the pre-

13. *Séminaire XI*, p. 180.
14. *Séminaire II*, p. 368.

dominance of the Imaginary in our culture results in a reification of the natural and ecosystemic relations between human beings—. . . the conversion of interdependent similarities and differences (between 'man' and 'woman,' for example) into pathological identities and oppositions (as between the IMAGES of man and woman in our culture)."[15] An awareness of the Symbolic order can therefore be seen as a corrective, because it promulgates notions of exchange and reciprocity; it introduces relativity and reversibility in value systems that have solidified in the Imaginary; and it founds the subject's existence in the context of a relation with the Other, not in the name of a truth. From a purely Symbolic perspective, the functioning of humans acquires an essentially mechanistic character and, as Lacan has pointed out, since it is devoid of consciousness, it is the machine that "incarnates the most radical symbolic activity in man."[16] In this sense, humans are no more than homeostatic mechanisms and humanisms are but momentary and contingent cohesions of sense perceptions. They are like pieces of tapestry constantly woven and rewoven, since they always unravel: the subject they intend to portray finds himself inevitably dispossessed of his truth by the Symbolic, which forces him to confront the reality of what is neither true nor false—of what "confers meaning on the function of the individual,"[17] which is the reality of language.

Since the reality of the subject is produced by discourse, it is necessarily transindividual; the question of the subject thus in effect concerns the story of his history—precisely and only because this story is kept hidden from him: as Lacan explains, "his life is oriented by a problematic which is not that of his life-experience [son vécu], but that of his destiny, that is to say—what is the meaning of his story/

15. Anthony Wilden, *System and Structure* (London: Tavistock, 1972), p. 19.
16. *Séminaire II*, p. 95.
17. *The Language of the Self*, p. 19.

37

history?"[18] It is a question that is equally important for Michel Foucault, who also endeavors to analyze man's fundamental failure to understand his own history and attempts to show how this failure affects his existence. In order to realize this project, Foucault has found it necessary "to dispense with the constituent subject, to get rid of the subject itself, that's to say, to arrive at an analysis which can account for the constitution of the subject within a historical framework" (*PK*, p. 117). The truth of a subject finds itself displaced from an inner subjective certitude to the realm of a discourse that is seen to exist in terms of a historical contingency; thus, an appropriate approach to the problem of truth in general "does not consist in drawing the line between that in a discourse which falls under the category of scientificity or truth, and that which comes under some other category, but in seeing historically how effects of truth are produced within discourses which in themselves are neither true nor false" (*PK*, p. 118). In showing that Western man is subject to determinisms that transcend his consciousness of an identity, Foucault, in effect, assumes the role of psychoanalyst. His purpose is comparable to Lacan's, since it also consists in showing that "man is not an object, but a being in the process of realizing itself, something metaphysical,"[19] that our humanity is not the image we construe of ourselves but something over which we have little control. As a "practitioner of the Symbolic function," the analyst aims to divest our Self of the privilege we derive from evidence that is nothing more than a historical happenstance, and to make us discover that our "syntax is linked to the dimension of the unconscious."[20] Foucault's writing has a similar effect, in that it problematizes the truths that a Western consciousness has developed around its own representation of itself and

18. *Séminaire II*, p. 58. The word *histoire* can mean both "story" and "history," whence the meaningful ambiguity of the question.

19. Ibid., p. 130.

20. *Séminaire XI*, p. 66.

brings out the dimension that has been instrumental in organizing Western discourse.

Finally, and still in the context of the subject, the question of Foucault's own status as the subject *in* and *of* his discourse inevitably arises. Here the analogy of the analyst can be dangerously misleading, since it could entice us into positing Foucault as the mirror or the alter ego of Western discourse. The relationship, however, is not a symmetrical one, and to objectify Foucault by making him into the subject of his own discourse would amount to adopting a strategy of interpretation that Foucault specifically intends to discredit. He has shown for example that the traditional notion of author is a convenient explanatory device, an a priori principle with which we are able to recuperate, to domesticate a text for our own specific purposes (*LCMP*, pp. 113–38). Furthermore, he has frequently reiterated his wish to minimize his own authorial presence in his work as much as possible. His comment on *Les mots et les choses* is characteristic of this attitude: "My book is pure and simple fiction: it is a novel, but I am not the one who has invented it, it is the relation of our era and of its epistemological configuration with this whole mass of statements. So that the subject is indeed present in the totality of the book, but he is the anonymous *'on'* that speaks today in everything that is said."[21] Since Foucault sees himself inextricably caught in a dimension that determines his own possibility of knowing and saying, his discourse is often tentative, even vague, in its prolixity; but because his discourse is groping in the area of darkness that masks the very foundations of its reality, it must necessarily be evocative rather than conclusive or authoritative. Foucault's desire to eliminate his own subjective presence from his work is attributable, then, to an attempt to reach those recesses of discourse that conceal its fundamental organizing principle. In trying to delineate the realm of the invisible yet

21. Raymond Bellour, *Le livre des autres* (Paris: Union Générale d'Editions, 1976), p. 110.

ever-present system that grants discourses their validity as statements of truth, Foucault grounds his writing not in the claim of an Imaginary, authorial creation, but in the awareness of the Symbolic—the silent void against which we are able to constitute our meanings.

2

An Archaeology of Silences

The dimension of the Symbolic precedes all empirical experience of reality; it is what makes such experience possible while keeping it from ever becoming a definitive representation of reality. An awareness of this Symbolic dimension will inevitably undermine the claims of any systematic and "objective" reconstruction of the human experience: "Man speaks therefore, but it is because the symbol has made him man."[1] Foucault sees this awareness as an inherently critical impulse, one that characterizes the fields of psychoanalysis and ethnology in particular, "not because they reach down to what is below consciousness in man, but because they are directed towards that which, outside man, makes it possible to know, with a positive knowledge, that which is given to or eludes his consciousness" (*OT*, p. 378). It is in this sense that they are sciences of the unconscious and it is in this sense that Foucault's own investigations carry forward their critical strategy, seeking to analyze man's discourse as something that mediates between his Other and the Self it manages to reconstruct. Foucault's archaeology does not seize upon the meanings or the images generated by discourse but brings to light all that is conspicuous by its absence, the areas of silence that are outlined when a discourse purports

1. Lacan, *The Language of the Self* (Baltimore: The Johns Hopkins University Press, 1953), p. 39.

to represent essences and truths. Consequently, it is the being of man's nonbeing—unreason and death—which can be seen to constitute the particular field of human experience Foucault investigates in his first two major publications: his *Histoire de la folie à l'âge classique* and *The Birth of the Clinic*.[2]

The book on insanity is not a history in the ordinary sense but, as Foucault notes in the conclusion, "a history of that which has made possible the very appearance of a psychology" (*HF*, p. 548). It does not reproduce a chronology of discoveries or a history of ideas but traces "the concatenation of fundamental structures of experience." Thus, the beginnings of a Western experience of madness are to be found in the area vacated by leprosy toward the end of the Middle Ages. It was an area that continued to support various rites of purification and exclusion while filling up with a strange new population of "vagabonds, criminals, and 'deranged minds,'" individuals who became the new subjects of "social exclusion but spiritual reintegration" (*MC*, p. 7; *HF*, p. 16). This strange and disquieting territory was also a region that both eluded human understanding and resisted the orderly processes of socialization. As a consequence, and at a very early stage in the constitution of a field of perception that can be termed "madness," there developed an opposition between a cosmic or tragic apprehension of insanity and a critical one—that is, one which strove to place madness within the confines of rational thought by producing a critique of madness. The cosmic attitude was informed by a sense of fascination and awe before the mystery of a universe beyond human comprehension, before the enigma of a world given to us by primitive forms of revelation: madness was seen as an opening to the secrets of a Symbolic dimen-

2. The English translation of *Histoire de la folie* includes only certain parts of the original and, from my perspective, the least interesting ones. I identify only the French version (*HF*) when the translation is mine and both versions when I quote from the English edition (*MC*).

sion. On the other hand, evolving in the wake of the humanistic tradition, the critical experience of madness quickly became the prevalent mode of approach to an area that eluded forms of rational discernment. It manifested itself in a discursive practice that sought to explain, to regulate, to sanction—thereby reducing everything beyond the humanly understandable to the norms and rules of a dominant morality. As the established dogma in the realm of ethics, Christianity recuperated madness in the name of the highest truth of this world and reduced it to the Imaginary dimension of a humanly controllable and rationally verifiable domain. Since religion wanted to reserve the area of the Symbolic strictly for itself, it inevitably sought to subject madness to rational control, thereby circumscribing it and, indeed, reducing it to silence.

Madness thus became the silence of reason and, for Foucault, this circumscription of an area that represents the impossibility of thought marks the advent of the Age of Reason, an age in which knowledge was to define itself with respect to ignorance and humanity in terms of the inhuman. This great machinery of truth called Reason, with its territorial claims over humanity, thus set up the boundaries separating truth from falsehood, reason from unreason. But because the Age of Reason was inevitably and inextricably involved in strategies already established by the church, it also erected the boundaries between good and evil—thus confusing from the very beginning its *ratio* with its *ethos* by elevating knowledge to the privileged position of a morality. Furthermore, this event made possible the alienation of man: it became possible to separate man from the truth, to consider and set him apart from it. Foucault therefore links the practice of confinement that began in the seventeenth century with the epistemological pattern underlying the so-called classical age. The royal decree of 1657 creating the Hôpital Général in Paris marks the beginning of a radically new relation between madness and reason:

If this decree with which modern man designated in the madman his own *alienated* truth has a meaning, it is the extent to
which was constituted, long before the madman took possession of it and symbolized it, this field of alienation to which he
was banished, along with so many other figures which, from
our standpoint, are no longer connected with him. This field
was actually delineated by the space of internment; and the
manner in which it was formed should indicate to us the manner in which the experience of madness was constituted. [*HF*,
p. 94]

The reconstruction of this experience makes up in effect an
archaeology of alienation and, at the same time that he highlights the discursive strategies of a culture seeking to justify
its procedures of banishment and social exclusion, Foucault
outlines the patterns of economic, social, and institutional
practices in which these strategies articulated themselves.

From an archaeological perspective, the practice of confinement becomes the realization of an axiological intention
to segregate all those who fail to meet certain social standards
and whose failure to conform makes them subject to a fundamentally moral condemnation: "Anyone interned is placed
within the field of this ethical valorization—and long before
being an object of knowledge or of pity, he is treated as a
moral subject (*HF*, p. 73). This ethical valorization serves to
explain, for us, the coherence of a perception—the understanding that made it possible to identify the misfit, to brand
the stranger, the one who had estranged himself from the
civilized world, since, in addition to the madman, the alienated included a rather surprising assortment of categories
such as the poor, beggars and invalids, and also the morally
reprehensible—syphilitics, prostitutes, debauchees and de-
bauchers, spendthrift fathers and prodigal sons, blasphemers,
libertines, homosexuals, alchemists. The treatments applied
were intended to punish, purify, and cure all at once and
involved an odd mixture of whippings, confessional rites,
penitence, and traditional medications. When medicine fi-

nally took over as the principal form of treatment for the insane, it had assimilated various aspects of the other methods. Very early, a complicity between medicine and morality had thus formed, and "our scientific and medical knowledge of madness rests implicitly on the earlier constitution of an ethical experience of unreason" (*HF*, p. 106).

While the eclipse of the Symbolic presence of unreason had helped to validate various rational approaches—critical, practical, rhetorical, and analytical approaches, to be specific— unreason had by no means been eliminated. Its mode of existence, however, had been profoundly altered: "Between Montaigne and Descartes an event took place: something which concerns the advent of a *ratio*. But the history of a *ratio* such as that of the Western world is far from exhausted by an account of the progress of a 'rationalism'; it is composed, to an equally great extent, of this secret movement by which Unreason buried itself in our ground, disappearing, of course, but also taking root in it" (*HF*, p. 58). At the same time, though unreason was driven underground, its status still remained ambiguous during the classical period. While attempting to exclude unreason, classical man also hoped to exorcise it, and while bringing it under control in the space of confinement, he also kept in mind the menace of its nihilistic presence: "For classical man, madness is not the natural condition, the human and psychological root of unreason; it is only its empirical form." Consequently, the presence of madness does not suggest to him a determinism inherent in the human condition, "but an opening towards darkness. More effectively than any other kind of rationalism, better in any case than our positivism, classical rationalism could watch out for and perceive the subterranean danger of unreason, that threatening space of an absolute freedom" (*MC*, pp. 83–84; *HF*, p. 175). Madness was connected both to a moral valorization of reason and to the "monstrous innocence" of unreason.

Madness was thus caught in a myth of unreason during

the classical age. With the advent of positivism in the nineteenth century, it becomes trapped in a myth of reason. A significant change takes place in the configuration of the Symbolic, the Imaginary, and the Real as the awareness of unreason that accompanied the perception of madness during the classical period is now replaced by Imaginary systems that will validate a modern interpretation of madness; and, although the procedure of confinement is still used, "by maintaining the madman in this situation of internment invented by the classical age, positivism will maintain him, without admitting this to itself, within the apparatus of moral constraint and of mastery over unreason" (*HF*, p. 177). This apparatus is not perceived as a mythical construct but accepted as the foundation of truth; thus, by equating the empirical with the ontological and refusing to question the validity of that procedure, positivism assumes the strategy characteristic of Imaginary processes. It now becomes possible to represent madness in "the serene and objective terms of *mental illness*" (*HF*, p. 182). But an even more important consequence of the tautological process established and justified by positivism is the recuperation of madness that has now been made possible in terms of the sane and the rational: in the classical age, it had been a question of "the dramatic constitution of a being following the violent suppression of his existence; now, within the serenity of knowledge, it is a question of constituting a nature following the unveiling of nonbeing" (*HF*, p. 191). Ironically, positivism is brought about by a negation which, Foucault maintains, "is even the first and the only *positive* phenomenon in the advent of *positivism*" (*HF*, p. 480). Within the context of positivism, madness makes possible the consciousness of not-being-mad and becomes thus "the first of the objectifying forms: that through which man can have an objective hold on himself" (*HF*, p. 481). Madness makes the truth of man amenable to objectification, thus making it accessible to an Imaginary mode of scientific perception.

It is a purely Imaginary mode of perception because it founds itself on a delusion that it systematically refuses to recognize. The first and most striking example of this delusion is the famous liberation of the insane at the very beginning of the nineteenth century by Philippe Pinel and Samuel Tuke, a doctor and a philanthropist who are credited with the introduction of a more humane and "scientific" treatment of madmen. The liberation, Foucault shows, was illusory: alienation had simply been interiorized. Although the insane had indeed lost their shackles, they were now held more securely than ever in the prison of their truth, a truth that emerged only because they had been suppressed as human beings. It was a truth that pertained to the being of *rational* man and the insane thus found themselves chained to a truth, a nature, a morality—in effect to reason. However, while it appeared that reason had at last conquered what had escaped it and had even threatened to disqualify it, the conquest turned out to be a Pyrrhic victory: not only was the *madman* a prisoner of this truth but the *sane* and *rational* man was one as well; as a consequence, "from this day, man has access to himself as a true being; but this true being is given to him only in the form of alienation" (*HF,* p. 548).

What the proponents of positivism failed to realize was that "reason alienates itself in the very movement by which it takes possession of unreason" (*HF,* p. 366). Reason had in effect become trapped in a strategy of its own making, and Foucault identifies the historical enabling condition of positivism as a confusion arising in the eighteenth century. He points out that in the classical period there had been two completely separate modes of dealing with unreason. On the one hand, the confinement of madmen was simply an effort to exclude unreason from the orderly and "reasonable" processes of society; on the other, there was an attempt to discover the "rational" truth of nature in the language and behavior of the insane. The two perspectives, inevitably

47

became confused and as a result of their superimposition there occurred a simultaneous exclusion and recuperation of madness: the one was made possible by the other since "reason immediately recognizes the negativity of the mad-man in the unreasonable, but recognizes itself in the rational contents of all madness" (*HF*, p. 203). This confusion was to lead to the muddled and pretentious strategy of positivism, for reason attempted to exclude and control what escaped it and at the same time wanted to define itself on the basis of this exclusion.

Foucault therefore sees the latter part of the eighteenth century as a crucial period of transition, a time when the fundamental epistemological configuration of the age was about to undergo a profound transformation. As reason set itself up in a position that would allow it to arrogate for itself the territories of both the Imaginary and the Symbolic and consequently to reproduce and interpret the Real with a clear conscience, unreason was driven underground and madness lost the power of its anguishing insights. Unreason became in fact the reason of reason—in a manner that we have just examined—and Foucault has discovered a remark-ably lucid witness to this momentous event in the central character of Diderot's *Le neveu de Rameau*. It seems fitting that a work that was never seen by Diderot's contemporaries should bear witness to a process of which these contem-poraries were equally unaware. Only our retrospective gaze is able to appreciate fully the profound insight offered by this text and, in a few pages that are among the most remark-able in his book, Foucault outlines the dramatic confrontation of reason, madness, and unreason that Rameau's nephew illustrates. What the character reveals, by acting out his per-ception of human reality and by impersonating a "delirium realized as existence, the delirium of the being and of the nonbeing of the Real," is the frailty of reason and the irony implicit in its pretension. Just before reason launched itself headlong into a forgetfulness of the ambiguities to which it owed its existence, this text by Diderot foreshadowed the course relations between reason and unreason would take:

> The laughter of Rameau's nephew prefigures and reduces in advance the whole anthropological movement of the nineteenth century; in all of post-Hegelian thought, man will proceed from certitude to truth through the efforts of the mind and reason; but already long before, Diderot had let it be understood that man is ceaselessly thrown back from reason to the untrue truth of the immediate, and this by means of an effortless mediation, a mediation always already operative since the beginning of time. This impatient mediation, which is both extreme distance and absolute promiscuity, entirely negative because it has only a subversive force, but completely positive, because it is fascinated by what it suppresses, this mediation is the delirium of unreason—the enigmatic figure in which we recognize madness. [*HF*, pp. 370–71]

Thereafter unreason would be forced to lead a subterranean existence, resurfacing only occasionally in the works of such rare figures as Hölderlin, Nerval, Nietzsche, Van Gogh, Raymond Roussel, and Artaud.[3] On the scientific side, it was Freud who would bring unreason to the fore once again and rediscover it as something not implicitly dependent on reason. This discovery, in Foucault's eyes, constitutes the great merit of Freud who, by dealing with madness "at the level of its *language,* reconstituted one of the essential elements of an experience reduced to silence by positivism; . . . he restored, in medical thought, the possibility of a dialogue with unreason" (*MC*, p. 198; *HF*, p. 360). And yet, while Foucault credits Freud with the revelation of an expe-

3. These figures have always exerted a conspicuous attraction for Foucault, and their names recur frequently in his works. Indeed, soon after the appearance of *Histoire de la folie,* he published *Raymond Roussel* (Paris: Gallimard, 1963). It is primarily a study of Roussel's language and style and brings out Foucault's fascination with a language that "comes to us from the depths of a night that is perfectly clear and impossible to dominate," a language that exists against the void that it inevitably and constantly produces (pp. 54, 207, 208).

49

rience that psychiatry before him had attempted to suppress and hide, he also detects in Freud's system the seeds of what would vitiate the psychoanalytic enterprise. Thus, although Freud indeed undermined some of the structures that had been put in place with the creation of the asylum, he maintained and even fortified one of them: "He abolished silence and observation, he eliminated madness's recognition of itself in the mirror of its own spectacle, he silenced the instances of condemnation. But on the other hand he exploited the structure that enveloped the medical personage; he amplified its thaumaturgical virtues, preparing for its omnipotence a quasi-divine status" (*MC*, p. 277; *HF*, p. 529). Freud not only helped to perpetuate the illusory myth of objectivity within which psychiatric knowledge had operated during the nineteenth century, he invested the personage of the doctor with all of the "massive structures of bourgeois society and its values: Family-Child relations, centered on the theme of paternal authority; Transgression-Punishment relations, centered on the theme of immediate justice; Madness-Disorder relations, centered on the theme of social and moral order" (*MC*, p. 274; *HF*, pp. 526–27). The psychoanalytical role of a doctor being Symbolic in nature—from the patient's point of view—the doctor who is intent on practicing a positive science inevitably engages in an Imaginary strategy that promulgates an ethic constructed by reason. Just as inevitably, however, any pretense of establishing Imaginary truths succumbs to an ultimate irony, to a "ruse and new triumph of madness: the world that thought to measure and justify madness through psychology must justify itself before madness, since in its struggles and agonies it measures itself by the excesses of works like those of Nietzsche, of Van Gogh, of Artaud. And nothing in itself, especially not what it can know of madness, assures the world that it is justified by such works of madness" (*MC*, p. 289; *HF*, p. 557). As an attempt to establish a science of man, psychoanalysis is therefore doomed to failure. From Foucault's standpoint, it is not a valid practice unless it serves to maintain an awareness of the Symbolic dimension in man's existence, of the void constituted by his death, his desire, and his language. It is a void against which man ceaselessly constructs his images of himself only to see them break up in the presence of this region that makes his images and his knowledge possible.

Psychoanalysis can thus redeem itself every time it works to subvert its own Imaginary procedures. In this regard, it represents a salutary tendency in the realm of psychiatry.[4] The science of medicine, on the other hand, presents a rich potential source of materials for an archaeological investigation precisely because it illustrates the opposite tendency: it has been instrumental in the formation of the human sciences —all those fields of knowledge that appeared within the Imaginary configuration of positivism. What Foucault wishes to investigate specifically in *The Birth of the Clinic,* is all that has supported medical discourse, the circumstances that have made it possible, that is, "the silent configuration in which language finds support: the relation of situation and attitude to what is speaking and what is spoken about" (*BC,* p. xi). This "Archaeology of Medical Perception" covers a relatively short span of time, the latter part of the eighteenth century and the first half of the nineteenth. It is, nevertheless, a crucial period, since it witnesses the emergence of modern medicine and of its specific mode of practice.

The strategy Foucault employs in *The Birth of the Clinic* is similar to that used in his history of madness: he does not start at the level of theoretical conceptualization in order to reconstruct the history of concepts but seeks to define the silent experience that allowed for the formation of certain institutionalized discourses and practices, the social conditions, the cultural structures and spaces that made possible

4. Such a strategy seems to be precisely the kind exemplified by the work of Lacan—which would therefore represent a successful intellectual enterprise from an archaeological viewpoint.

"a new alliance between words and things" in the realm of medicine. His inquiry is directed toward a prediscursive realm in the organization of discourse, "the region where 'things' and 'words' have not yet been separated, and where—at the most fundamental level of language—seeing and saying are still one" (*BC*, p. xi). An archaeological analysis intends to go beyond, or rather beneath the level of meanings and contents in an attempt to reach more fundamental mechanisms, because "what counts in the things said by men is not so much what they may have thought or the extent to which these things represent their thoughts, as that which systematizes them from the outset, thus making them thereafter endlessly accessible to new discourses and open to the task of transforming them" (*BC*, p. xix). In the case of medicine, such a fundamental causal role is enacted by the gaze. It is the profound transformation in the manner in which doctors *saw* the objects of their science that, for Foucault, accounts for the radical change in the practice of medicine. Furthermore, the fact that we are now in a position to identify such an event may be an indication of a recent or current transformation in these deeper epistemological determinants, an indication that we are no longer subject to the same prediscursive arrangement that determined systems of knowledge in the nineteenth century.

The very choice of the gaze as a subject of research is a strategic step, allowing Foucault to identify the a priori of the gaze: not only the historical conditions of possibility, but all the social, economic, technological, and institutional forces that contributed to shape a particular experience of the gaze. Although in his study of madness the principal emphasis was placed on the ethical foundations of psychiatry, in *The Birth of the Clinic*, Foucault brings out the political affiliations of knowledge and highlights the "spontaneous and deeply rooted convergence between the requirements of *political ideology* and those of *medical technology*" (*BC*, p. 38). Thus science and capitalism have both been "interested" in

the development of clinical medicine: "In a regime of economic freedom, the hospital had found a way of interesting
the rich; the clinic constitutes the progressive reversal of the
other contractual part; it is the *interest* paid by the poor on
the capital that the rich have consented to invest in the
hospital; an interest that must be understood in its heavy
surcharge, since it is a compensation that is of the order of
objective interest for science and of *vital interest* for the rich"
(*BC*, p. 85). Such collusions are of course never indicated in
the scientific language of medicine, which is a system of
knowledge purporting adequately to represent the reality of
bodies. Foucault demonstrates, however, that ever since the
time of Hippocrates medicine has been haunted by a metaphysics and, in this regard, medical and philosophical languages are identical in their deployment of an Imaginary
strategy intended to capture the Real; they both thrive in a
mode "in which the visible and the manifest come together
in at least a virtual identity, in which the perceived and the
perceptible may be wholly restored in a language whose
rigorous form declares its origin. The doctor's discursive,
reflective perception and the philospher's discursive reflex-
ion on perception come together in a figure of exact super-
position, since *the world is for them the analogue of language*"
(*BC*, p. 96). This language is what supplements the silence
of the gaze in medicine but fails to reveal the extent to which
that silence has already been structured in advance and made
receptive to a particular form of language; it is a gaze that
has already formed its own syntax.

The beginning student of medicine is taught to assume an
inherently innocent gaze. He deals with symptoms, with the
evidence of disease, as if they were readily available to the
perceptive eye: in fact, "it is not the gaze itself that has the
power of analysis and synthesis, but the synthetic truth of
language, which is added from the outside, as a reward for
the vigilant gaze of the student" (*BC*, p. 60). There are codes
of knowledge binding the gaze to the field of perception,

and a symptom is not an evidence in and of itself since "it can receive its meaning only from an earlier act that does not belong to its sphere: from an act that totalizes and isolates it, that is, from an act that has transformed it into a sign in advance" (*BC*, p. 92). Foucault finds that, in addition to obscuring this constitutive act, medical discourse has also concealed the reductive process that has permitted medicine to develop its theoretical field: it is a process whose purpose has been to reconcile the insufficiency and extreme scantiness of medical theory with the overwhelming complexity of its object—the human body. In order to bring about such a reconciliation, medical science has discovered an effective strategy, thanks to which the poverty of ignorance has been turned into the plenitude of knowledge: "Medicine discovered that uncertainty may be treated, analytically, as the sum of a certain number of isolatable degrees of certainty that were capable of rigorous calculation" (*BC*, p. 97). Foucault thus reveals that the epistemological design of medical science, as it emerges in its modern form, fits into the overall pattern of positivism with its anthropocentric self-sufficiency. An archaeological perusal of the gaze allows him to reconstruct the economies of scientific and political interest that have supported its silence and lets him identify the critical elements contributing to the sudden transformation of medical perception.

The constitution of modern anatomo-clinical medicine is brought about, generally speaking, by a modification in the "general arrangement of knowledge that determines the reciprocal positions and the connexion between the one who must know and that which is to be known" (*BC*, p. 137). Specifically, it is the dissection of corpses that produces this fundamental change as a result of which "the medical gaze pivots on itself and demands of death an account of life and disease" (*BC*, p. 146). In the case of madness, unreason was made to account for reason and was thereby entirely called back within the space of reason; similarly, the anatomopathological science of medicine constitutes death as the foundation of knowledge, thus making life into a prefiguration of death. Death becomes "disease made possible in life" (*BC*, p. 156). Death as the Other is reduced to the Same which, at the same time, becomes alienated from itself since life is now made perceptible in a lifeless inertness: pathological anatomy "substitutes for a methodology of the visible a more complex experience in which truth emerges from its inaccessible reserve only in the passage to the inert, to the violence of the dissected corpse, and hence to forms in which living signification withdraws in favor of a massive geometry" (*BC*, p. 159). In a sense, life has become transparent, thus revealing the overwhelming yet invisible presence of death. The obscurity of life is overcome by the light of a "limpid death" and, in this sense, medical gaze can be seen from the perspective of an irreducible paradox: Foucault finds that "the structure, at once perceptual and epistemological, that commands clinical anatomy, and all medicine that derives from it, is that of *invisible visibility*" (*BC*, p. 165).

It is, of course, questionable whether such concepts as "invisible visibility" can take us very far toward understanding cultural phenomena, and one can argue that the whole notion of the gaze is a rather shaky and nebulous one to begin with. In this respect, *The Birth of the Clinic* is perhaps not as successful as other works, and Foucault was to discard the concept of the gaze in his later studies. Nevertheless, by examining a relatively brief episode in the history of medicine from such a perspective, he was able, in *The Birth of the Clinic*, to outline more precisely the pattern of thought he had adumbrated in the history of madness—a configuration that would become a major subject of investigation in subsequent works. It is the pattern that made it possible for man to become an object of positive knowledge. Following the epistemological upheaval that was signaled by the emergence of modern psychiatry and clinical medicine, man's existence was to be appropriated by a finitude that became simultaneously the object and the foundation of his knowledge. While in classical thought, finitude had simply been the negation of the infinite, toward the end of the eighteenth century it acquired a positive force. As a consequence, "the anthropological structure that then appeared played both the critical role of limit and the founding role of origin." It is in this context, in relation to the "over-all architecture of the human sciences" that Foucault examines medicine since, for him, "it is closer than any of them to the anthropological structures that sustain them all" (*BC*, pp. 197–98).

But medicine also reveals a basic feeling of inadequacy inevitably generated by a reliance on Imaginary structures. Medicine is exemplary of the inescapable anguish that undermines all anthropologically motivated explanations of man, all the images of humanity that allow for the constitution of clearly demarcated individualities. Thus, it is precisely because medicine is a "science of the individual" that it provides a dramatic illustration of what Foucault considers an essential characteristic of our culture, the fact that "the individual owes to death a meaning that does not cease with him. The division that it traces and the finitude whose mark it imposes link, paradoxically, the universality of language and the precarious, irreplaceable form of the individual" (*BC*, p. 197). Death and language both partake of the Imaginary and the Symbolic: death and language limit the meaning of individuals, yet also impose a meaning that is already there before us, in spite of us, a meaning in which we seek to justify our individuality but one which constantly undermines all our efforts by exposing their inadequacy. *The Birth of the Clinic* can thus serve to locate Foucault's critical enterprise within this fundamental paradox, since it clearly brings out the concerns that were to motivate his archaeological investigations in the work that followed. We have seen that with *Histoire de la folie* Foucault's archaeological strategy manifested certain affinities with psychoanalytical and ethnological modes of investigation; in *The Birth of the Clinic* Foucault highlights a third field, pointing out that

> for Kant, the possibility and necessity of a critique were linked, through certain scientific contents, to the fact that there is such a thing as knowledge. In our time—and Nietzsche the philologist testifies to it—they are linked to the fact that language exists and that, in the innumerable words spoken by men—whether they are reasonable or senseless, demonstrative or poetic—a meaning has taken shape that hangs over us, leading us forward in our blindness, but awaiting in the darkness for us to attain awareness before emerging into the light of day and speaking. [*BC*, pp. xv–xvi]

For Foucault, the possibility and necessity of a critique is linked to the realization that our very humanity is not so much an ontological given as an epistemological construct—that the image of man perceptible in our discourses perhaps owes its existence to something beyond our control and that the very notion of man can be considered separately from the discursive dimension in which it is given. The being of man and the representation of man become clearly separate issues once we consider discursive and cognitive functions of language, once we raise the question of discourse, of its ontological privilege and epistemological powers.

3

The Uses of an *Episteme*

Man exists, then, as an element of discourse. Since this existence is due to a radical change in the epistemological configuration of Western discourse, man is simply to be viewed as the product of a historical contingency; and although we may find it difficult to imagine this, Foucault reminds us that there was a time "when the world, its order, and human beings existed, but man did not." Our thinking has been conditioned by forces beyond our conscious control and we "believe ourselves bound to a finitude which belongs only to us, and which opens up the truth of the world to us by means of our cognition" (*OT*, p. 322). This illusory mode of producing the truth about ourselves and the world characterizes, as we have seen, an anthropological process and is a function of the *episteme* that governs our mode of cognition.

The *episteme* is one of the more problematic concepts that Foucault has developed, yet it is an indispensable element of his archaeology.[1] It is a notion that partakes of the Symbolic

1. Foucault's notion of the *episteme* has probably attracted more negative criticism than any other aspect of his methodology and for understandable reasons: it posits certain periodic totalities, supposes a structure of invisible epistemological determinisms, and does not allow for effects of causality or continuity. See for example George Huppert, "*Divinatio et Eruditio*: Thoughts on Foucault," *History and Theory* 8 (1974), 191–207, in which the author demonstrates that Foucault has seriously misrepresented the sixteenth cen-

order—manifesting itself as both an inescapable and an in-tangible domain of determinisms which constitute what Fou-cault calls the "positive unconscious of knowledge." It rep-resents a field of epistemological possibilities structured in a way that will determine the particular mode in which knowl-edge is to be achieved in a given culture and age. The area of the *episteme* is designated as a sort of "middle region" that exists between the already "encoded eye" and reflexive language, that is to say, between the two distinct conscious movements that mark a subject's quest for knowledge: there is the initial decision that delineates a field of observation or experimentation—a decision already motivated by cultural determinants—and there is the act of reflection that seeks to integrate the results of observation or experimentation with-in the framework of accumulated knowledge. The process would be perfectly circular were it not for the intervention of this unconscious mediation:

> This middle region, then, in so far as it makes manifest the modes of being of order, can be posited as the most funda-mental of all: anterior to words, perceptions, and gestures, which are then taken to be more or less exact, more or less happy expressions of it (which is why this experience of order in its pure primary state always plays a critical role); more solid, more archaic, less dubious, always more "true" than the theories that attempt to give those expressions explicit form, exhaustive application, or philosophical foundation. Thus, in every culture, between the use of what one might call the ordering codes and reflections upon order itself, there is the pure experience of order and of its modes of being. [*OT*, p. xxi]

This awareness of a "pure experience of order" that Foucault wishes to impart in *The Order of Things* is a basic strategic device in his work: it has the effect of producing a shift

---

tury. See also Jan Miel, "Ideas or Epistemes: Hazard Versus Foucault," *Yale French Studies* 49 (1973), 231–245.

in our perception—away from the objects of discourse and toward the system of prediscursive relations that make discourse possible, "the epistemological field, the *episteme* in which knowledge, envisaged apart from all criteria having reference to its rational value or to its objective forms, grounds its positivity and thereby manifests a history which is not that of its growing perfection, but rather that of its conditions of possibility" (*OT*, p. xxii). Of course, the *episteme* is irreducible to concrete experience and is therefore not amenable to a systematic description. It can only be posited— but even this limited theoretical possibility is of considerable benefit for an investigation of discourse, because the realm of order that finds itself hypothesized in this manner brings with it the perspective of the Symbolic: it presents itself as a realm that can both impose and liberate order; and if, following Lacan, we take discourse to be "a process of language which compels and constrains truth,"[2] then, by allowing for an epistemological mediation of the Symbolic, we gain the understanding that "truth is a thing of this world: it is produced only by virtue of multiple forms of constraint" (*PK*, p. 131).

Truth, we have already seen, is made possible by the Imaginary dimension. Accordingly, it is at the level of the Imaginary that concrete manifestations of the *episteme* occur. Indeed, the epistemological configuration of Western discourse formed in the nineteenth century manifests the delusive character of the Imaginary mode: man's knowledge of himself is based on the image he produces of himself and is grounded in his experience of his own body, desire, and language. Analyzing the disciplines of philology, biology, and economics to reveal certain regularities in the codification of Western systems of knowledge, Foucault also outlines the being of man as the ontological product of an analytic of finitude. Within the epistemological constraints of this an-

---

2. Quoted by Wilden in *The Language of the Self*, p. xxiv.

alytic, man realizes himself by basing the transcendental status of his knowledge on the ground of an experience of limits that is taken to be the very foundation of his being:

> At the foundation of all empirical positivities, and of every-thing that can indicate itself as a concrete limitation of man's existence, we discover a finitude—which is in a sense the same: it is marked by the spaciality of the body, the yawning of desire, and the time of language; yet it is radically other: in this sense, the limitation is expressed not as a determination im-posed upon man from the outside (because he has a nature or a history), but as a fundamental finitude which rests on nothing but its own existence as fact, and opens upon the positivity of all concrete limitation.   [*OT*, p. 315]

The epistemological shift that makes the production of knowl-edge derivative of an analytic of finitude inaugurates the reign of a sovereign consciousness. It is an era in which man, appearing as "a strange empirico-transcendental dou-blet," takes himself to be not only the origin and foundation of all knowledge but, more important, a self-sufficient con-sciousness able to guarantee the truth of this knowledge. It is, characteristically, an era thoroughly dominated by the Imaginary: the configuration of the three orders of percep-tion tends to be constantly reduced to a bi-polar interaction between the Imaginary and the Real. The occlusion of the Symbolic occurs in two principal ways: in one case, man is granted an ability to determine truth and beauty that is somehow inherent in his very nature; this transcendental nature has the potential to fuse his inner world of percep-tion with the world outside, giving rise to what Foucault calls a "transcendental aesthetic." In the other case, man discovers the truth of his being in his own history and finds his existence determined by a past that he takes to be the guarantor of humanity's destiny; the latter approach has pro-duced a "transcendental dialectic." Both types of analysis "claim to be able to rest entirely on themselves, since it is

the contents themselves that function as transcendental reflection" (*OT*, p. 319); thus predicated on a collusion between the Imaginary and the Real, they are part of an anthropological pattern centered on a constituent subject.

Specifically, this pattern characterizes the major philosophical modes to have evolved from the nineteenth century.
Thus, phenomenology is a basically vitiated system "which
gives absolute priority to the observing subject, which attributes a constituent role to an act, which places its own
point of view at the origin of all historicity—which, in short,
leads to a transcendental consciousness" (*OT*, p. xiv). Also
discredited are such fundamentally naïve forms of philosophical reflection as positivism and Marxism, these being
modes of thought whose effectiveness is attributable to an
intellectual sleight of hand, since, for them, the "pre-critical
analysis of what man is in his essence becomes the analytic
of everything that can, in general, be presented to man's
experience." The act of observing is taken to lie at the origin
of all reflection, to be the pristine and uncontaminated source
of all knowledge; the empirical and critical functions are
fused into one: the scientific pretense of Marxism and positivism is based on a strategy that consists of "an empirico-
critical reduplication by means of which an attempt is made
to make the man of nature, of exchange, or of discourse,
serve as the foundation of his own finitude" (*OT*, p. 341).
Positivism achieves credibility by granting a transcendental
status to man's immediate perception of the Real and predi-
cates the validity of its discourse on the truth of the object:
it is a discourse that rejects the mediation of the Symbolic
from the outset. On the other hand, eschatological discourse
not only elides the Symbolic by reducing it to a system of
material determinisms, but even manifests a tendency to
weld the Imaginary to the Real in an indissoluble paradigm:
Marxist discourse is true because it is reality itself, it is the
Word incarnate. In both cases, there is a blindness toward
those crucial determinisms that are irreducible to discourse

and that are always already in place, and "a discourse attempting to be both empirical and critical cannot but be both positivist and eschatological; man appears within it as a truth both reduced and promised. Pre-critical naïveté holds undivided rule" (*OT*, p. 320). Instead of truth then, we have a profound misunderstanding concerning the manner in which truth is produced.[3]

Since the modern *episteme* is sustained by this sort of misunderstanding, it stands to reason that it should make a powerful contribution to maintaining the latter. In effect, it imposes its order by dint of a methodical misunderstanding of the Symbolic, by cultivating a form of self-deception that results in the eclipse of the Symbolic order of perception. Such a strategy fails to eliminate the Symbolic, of course, but has instead produced a pervasive malaise, a feeling of instability that constantly undermines the certainty man wishes to establish around his existence: "Man has not been able to describe himself as a configuration in the *episteme* without thought at the same time discovering, both in itself and outside itself, at its borders yet also in its very warp and woof, an element of darkness, an apparently inert density in which it is embedded, an unthought which it contains entirely, yet in which it is also caught" (*OT*, p. 326). Yet, while recognizing the realm of the Symbolic, Western man has been unwilling to grant it the autonomy and sovereignty its function implies. The impulse characteristic of the modern *episteme* has been to recuperate, to colonize, to disenfranchise the Symbolic in the name of a *ratio*. Man utilizes the Symbolic to reinforce, to support the Imaginary, thus giving rise to a form of knowledge that is sustained by a will to appropriate and to dominate. Modern Western thought is to be viewed, then, as a purposeful and aggressive mode of action, since "whatever it touches it immediately causes to

3. Foucault's attitude toward Marxism is, of course, not as simple as these examples make it appear. Chapter 8 provides a fuller discussion of this particular aspect of Foucault's thought.

move: it cannot discover the unthought, or at least move towards it, without immediately bringing the unthought nearer to itself—or even, perhaps, without pushing it further away, and in any case without causing man's own being to undergo a change by that very fact, since it is deployed in the distance between them" (*OT*, p. 327). Man's existence in the modern *episteme* is therefore predicated on a refusal to accept the Other, the Symbolic for what it is: a refusal to see it as the inaccessible, ineffable presence that renders man insignificant, that makes the subject disintegrate, that undermines man's pretense to establish control over "his" world. The Other is recognized only to be reincorporated within the boundaries overseen by the Imaginary; the Symbolic is admitted only to be domesticated, to be gradually eroded in order to safeguard the substance of the subject in Western discourse, to preserve the subject's privilege of determining his own truth.

In an anthropological configuration of knowledge, man has an epistemological consciousness of himself in the sense that he takes himself to be the basis for all his knowledge; at the same time, he is not truly conscious of this consciousness and, what is more important, he is not conscious of the endless deceit involved in his confident strategy of making his knowledge identical with it. Foucault bases his critique on the paradoxical understanding that an *episteme* predicated on an analytic of finitude is not identical with itself. The *episteme* produces a form of knowledge that espouses the predetermined forms and epistemological patterns derived from the Symbolic; yet, while this knowledge may very well recognize its own configuration in terms of an analytic of finitude, it fails to take into account the purely contingent nature of the *episteme*. It takes the latter to be an absolute; that is to say, knowledge materializes as the conscious or Imaginary product of the *episteme*, it appears only on the conscious or Imaginary side of the *episteme*, thus eliding the Symbolic dimension. The *episteme* exists only by virtue of its capacity to produce a certain form of knowledge, yet this very knowledge comes into being only because it denies the essential aspect of its provenance: it hides the fact that it is based on the absence of any real foundation. The existence of the *episteme*, then, is founded on its nonexistence, it dissolves as soon as it is identified; as a concrete notion, it can function only as a critical instrument. It operates as an epistemological determinant so long as it remains invisible, so long as the purely arbitrary and happenstance nature of its arrangement remains undetected. As soon as its mechanisms are revealed against the background of the Symbolic as the uncontrollable designs of chance, its hold has been broken; that which resided at the level of the Symbolic has thereby been recuperated in the Imaginary, and a different configuration of unconscious strategies has already formed.

An effective critique of our culture must perforce begin at the level of the *episteme*. Indeed, the very act of positing a prediscursive economy puts the entire cultural establishment in question. Because of the extraordinary status enjoyed by knowledge in our civilization, because of the invariable pattern according to which "discursive formations are constantly becoming epistemologized" (*AK*, p. 195) in our culture, to suppose there is anything that takes precedence over processes of cognition is to question the very validity of the systems of knowledge that support our civilization. Knowledge formed under the aegis of an analytic of finitude is thus severely limited in its scope and consistently fails to bring up the sort of questions that take the Symbolic into account:

> How can man think what he does not think, inhabit as though by a mute occupation something that eludes him, animate with a kind of frozen movement that figure of himself that takes the form of a stubborn exteriority? How can man *be* that life whose web, pulsations, and buried energy constantly exceed the experience that he is immediately given of them? How can he *be* that labour whose laws and demands are imposed upon him

like some alien system? How can he be the subject of a language that for thousands of years has been formed without him, a language whose organization escapes him, whose meaning sleeps an almost invincible sleep in the words he momentarily activates by means of discourse, and within which he is obliged, from the very outset, to lodge his speech and thought, as though they were doing no more than animate, for a brief period, one segment of that web of innumerable possibilities? [OT, p. 323]

The *episteme* is already one element that serves to suggest some answers to such questions, and Foucault presents it as the deep-seated regularity that determines the manner in which man organizes not only his systems of meaning, but also the relation he perceives between himself and his meanings. Yet the *episteme* is not an explanatory device, an entity that would serve to justify the existence of a particular discourse at a particular time; it is made to fit into Foucault's archaeological strategy, into the method of inquiry with which he seeks to unmake this "man" who has constituted his positivity in the human sciences, a man whose knowledge has been made possible by an *episteme* and whose reality is given by an archive.

4

The Archive and the Symbolic

At the same time that it extricates man from the discourses that have formed him, Foucault's archaeology also seeks to dispossess us of our discourses, or, more specifically, of all the familiar approaches with which we are accustomed to deal with discourse. The aim is to direct our thinking away from the internal "meaning" of a discourse to its external conditions of possibility, in order to suggest all the circumjacent factors outlining the space of a particular discourse and to indicate that the question to be asked is *why* "one particular statement appeared rather than another" (*AK*, p. 27). Such an approach effects a break with all the themes of interpretation that occur to us as natural, immediate, and universal elements of cognition. It is also intended to make the readers of *The Archaeology of Knowledge* understand that "their history, their economics, their social practices, the language (*langue*) that they speak, the mythology of their ancestors, even the stories that they were told in their childhood, are governed by rules that are not all given to their consciousness" (*AK*, pp. 210–11). Foucault's attempt to elaborate an "archaeology of knowledge" is thus oriented toward the Symbolic dimension that withholds these rules, toward all those generally unsuspected, invisible causative systems.

An archaeological approach has the distinct advantage of disrupting an Imaginary pattern of thought; it rejects, first of all, the themes of continuity and totality that have been the constitutive elements of traditional methodologies. Furthermore, it provides a radically changed perspective that suggests a concrete utilization of the Symbolic. It accomplishes this by considering discourse at a level that is alien to so-called humanistic interpretations, one that excludes meaning and marks the existence of discourse without reference to either words or things: "Of course, discourses are composed of signs; but what they do is more than use these signs to designate things. It is this *more* that renders them irreducible to language (*langue*) and to speech" (*AK*, p. 49). Neither is discourse referred to the plenitude of a sovereign consciousness because, from an archaeological perspective, "the time of discourse is not the translation, in a visible chronology, of the obscure time of thought" (*AK*, p. 122). Discourse is made to lose its contents, its referential dimension, its capacity to reflect the world and to represent a mind, and is constituted into a configuration of discursive objects—of elements whose domain is not content but an exteriority that precedes the conscious activity of a meaningful subjectivity.

The conventional links that have been used to connect a discourse either to the internal reality of an author or to a world of events and of time that it purports to represent are relations that provide explanations of causality and produce themes of continuity and unity in traditional modes. Transposed to the level of an archaeological analysis, they are not eliminated but become discursive objects themselves: they are seen as the products of a particular discursive practice that has made their function both necessary and effective. Links of causality are thus seen as projections of a certain anthropological thought that justifies their presence as legitimate explanatory devices and governs their use as valid elements of discourse.

The sort of causal factors that Foucault does recognize belong to the order of the Symbolic, since, in their mode of functioning, they are radically different from the connecting elements that obtain in the Imaginary. The latter are seen to determine the presence of certain objects in a discourse and therefore belong to these objects as their constitutive characteristics. Thus, in the Imaginary, the elements of a discourse inherently possess the power to reproduce reality; they can exist as extensions of the inner world of a subject or act as allegorical reflections of a world that is outside discourse. Foucault's archaeological determinants are neither internal to a discourse nor are they external constraints that impose specific forms or modes of existence on the discourse:

> They are, in a sense, at the limit of discourse: they offer it objects of which it can speak, or rather (for this image of offering presupposes that objects are formed independently of discourse), they determine the group of relations that discourse must establish in order to speak of this or that object, in order to deal with them, name them, analyze them, classify them, explain them, etc. These relations characterize not the language [*langue*] used by discourse, nor the circumstances in which it is deployed, but discourse itself as a practice. [*AK*, p. 46]

Being immanent in the discursive practice itself, such relations do not derive from elements that produce cohesiveness on an Imaginary level—notions of aesthetic unity such as "genre," psychological rationalizations such as "mentality" or "spirit of an age". They are relations that function on a level at which discourses are seen as events, where they are free from all categorizations that could be considered natural, immediate, and universal.

Considered on a purely discursive level, contents also become discursive objects. Discourse loses its referential depth, that mimetic dimension which is sustained by the inherent privilege it has always had to represent reality: "What, in short, we wish to do is to dispense with 'things.' To 'depresentify' them. To dissipate their rich, heavy immediate plenitude, which we usually regard as the primitive law of a discourse" (*AK*, p. 47).[1] Instead of viewing discourse from the outside, Foucault situates his point of view inside, as it were: to approach a discourse from the outside implies a strategy that aims to uncover, to dislodge, through interpretative or hermeneutical means, something the discourse withholds from immediate apprehension. A Foucaldian approach requires that we focus away from an Imaginary, anthropologically derived profundity and that we consider instead discourse as a surface, as a network of exchanges in a signifying field, as an interplay of discursive objects. Such a course allows us to reach a purely discursive level at which the constitutive elements of discourse appear as points in a network of signifying chains, not as meaningful signals pregnant with a content that is the reason for their existence. For an archaeological analysis, these elements exist because they have the capacity to carry meaning, because they are making a statement. What gives them their status of statement is the coalescence of circumstances in which they happen to arise as specific *énoncés*; it is the fact that an enunciative occurrence has taken place, producing a particular message as opposed to an infinity of other possibilities.[2]

It is this notion of *énoncé* or statement that contributes more than any other aspect of Foucault's theory to an apprehension of the Symbolic. The *énoncé* has a paradoxical mode of being, since it is "neither visible nor hidden" (*AK*, p. 109). It is primarily a function and as such it partakes of the peculiar nature of the Symbolic: it functions as an element in a system of communication, yet it is neither *what* it communi-

1. I note in passing that the English translation of this rather crucial passage is misleading: Sheridan uses "to conjure" which means "to summon," for *conjurer*, which should be "to drive away," "to dissipate."

2. Although "statement" is the proper term corresponding to *énoncé*, I prefer to use the French word because it is more precise in its meaning: it does not automatically imply, as does "statement," the notion of contents, of that which is stated; rather, *énoncé* suspends this notion and appears, at least momentarily, as *pure function*, which is precisely the aspect that Foucault wishes to analyze with regard to discourses.

cates nor *how* it communicates that matters, but the *fact that* it communicates. Neither Imaginary nor Symbolic, the *énoncé* is Real. The level of the *énoncé* is one at which language manifests itself in its "functional materiality," it is the level at which both signifier and signified are suspended: "Language, in its appearance and mode of being, is the statement; as such it belongs to a description that is neither transcendental nor anthropological" (*AK*, p. 113). At the same time, the *énoncé* evades any precise description because it is "always an event that neither language nor meaning can quite exhaust" (*AK*, p. 28). Since it belongs to neither the level of the signifier nor that of the signified, it escapes any sort of description derived from the perspective of these levels. Nevertheless, it does have a tangible existence: "In relation to all these descriptive approaches, it plays the role of a residual element, of a mere fact, of irrelevant, raw material" (*AK*, p. 84). As a signifying function, it makes certain fragments of meaning appear, but the signifying content it carries does not constitute its motivation or reason for being. The *énoncé* has its own conditions of possibility that are specific to its particular level. Neither causal nor inherent, the relations that sustain it are correlative: it is totally dependent upon a vast domain that establishes the conditions for its existence:

> It is linked . . . to a "referential" that is made up not of "things," "facts," "realities," or "beings," but of laws of possibility, rules of existence for the objects that are named, designated, or described within it, and for the relations that are affirmed or denied in it. The referential of the statement forms the place, the condition, the field of emergence, the authority to differentiate between individuals or objects, states of things and relations that are brought into play by the statement itself; it defines the possibilities of appearance and delimitation of that which gives meaning to the sentence, a value as truth to the proposition. It is this group that characterizes the *enunciative* level of the formulation, in contrast to its grammatical and logical levels: through the relation with these various domains

of possibility the statement makes of a syntagma, or a series of symbols, a sentence to which one may or may not ascribe a meaning, a proposition that may or may not be accorded a value as truth.   [*AK*, pp. 91–92]

Since the *énoncé* derives its importance from a network of causal factors, Foucault finds that what is important to describe is not the statement in itself (for the obvious reason that it is simply not available for description), but rather the enunciative field that actualizes the conditions necessary for the realization of enunciative functions. An archaeological analysis will therefore concern itself with a "field of dispersion," with the reality of things that are written and articulated, but it will consider them at the level that reveals their existence as singular discursive events, not as signs that stand for something else. Thus, to grasp this enunciative function, it becomes necessary to "question language, not in the direction to which it refers, but in the dimension that gives it" (*AK*, p. 111). Furthermore, the relationship uniting an *énoncé* to what is enunciated is to be distinguished from the signifier/signified rapport, which is maintained on the basis of an identification. The *énoncé* and the enunciated exist in a mutually exclusive mode. As a function, the *énoncé* remains invisible, though perceptible to a certain sense of understanding; the moment an enunciative function fulfills the minimum requirements necessary for giving a sign or a group of signs a specific meaning, a statement comes into being. However, as soon as a message is understood and its contents are perceived, the *énoncé* disappears behind the image it has brought forth—the enunciative function is inevitably obliterated by the Imaginary, without which, nevertheless, it would never have materialized. It is thus a relationship that is characteristic of the mutually exclusive and interdependent existence of the Imaginary and Symbolic orders.

Consequently, the archaeological perspective can be defined as an approach to discourses that is effectuated at the level of the *énoncé*. It is at this level that the elements of discourse will be analyzed as functions that serve to explain the appearance of a discourse as a specific event. An element such as the subject, for example, exists in the Imaginary mode as the possessor and producer of knowledge, as the synthesizing force able to project unto the world the coherence of his explanations; in Foucault's archaeology, the perspective offered by the *énoncé* deprives the subject of its integrative and causal privileges and presents discourse as a "field of regularity for various positions of subjectivity." As a result, "instead of referring back to *the* synthesis or *the* unifying function of *a* subject, the various enunciative modalities manifest his dispersion." From a Symbolic perspective, the subject loses both his status as "the pure founding authority of rationality" and his role as "an empirical function of synthesis" (*AK*, p. 54). The function of the subject is to be defined as an empty yet definite space that can be occupied by anyone becoming involved in a particular enunciative configuration. There exists also the possibility of various subjective positions that can be strategically occupied by the same subject assuming different roles. Since the *énoncé* derives its identity from a field of utilization in which it is actualized, its existence is dependent upon the specific position that a subject can take up in it. In the Symbolic mode, statements do not originate in the creative consciousness of a subject: they are activated in a configuration of possibilities the moment a subject engages in an enunciative field: the subject does not precede the statement but is coeval with it.

Just as the subject is demoted from the primary role it plays in the Imaginary to a dependent and secondary rank in the Symbolic, concepts lose their status of "truths" or "truthful insights" when considered on a purely discursive level. In the realm of enunciative modalities, concepts are determined by the relations that link statements; they lose the aura of an ideal origin. At this level, discourse is no longer understood as an external form that incorporates within its framework the concepts it decides to lift out from a pre-existing ideality. Discourse has become a surface on which concepts take shape according to a system of discursive regularities. These are forms of coexistence, relationships that discourses establish with other discourses, rapports that in turn allow for the appropriation, transformation, or rejection of various concepts. Under these circumstances, concepts are no longer considered as universally valid, applicable in various contexts by virtue of their truth-value. They are not even interesting in and of themselves and, for Foucault, the important task is not to study concepts for themselves, a task that involves a tautological or anthropological strategy, but to discern the articulations inherent in a conceptual field:

> One tries to determine according to what schemata (of series, simultaneous groupings, linear or reciprocal modification) statements may be linked to one another in a type of discourse; one tries in this way to discover how the recurrent elements of statements can reappear, dissociate, recompose, gain in extension or determination, be taken up into new logical structures, acquire, on the other hand, new semantic contents, and constitute partial organizations among themselves. These schemata make it possible to describe—not the laws of the internal construction of concepts, not their progressive and individual genesis in the mind of man—but their anonymous dispersion through texts, books, and *œuvres*. A dispersion that characterprizes a type of discourse, and which defines, between concepts, forms of deduction, derivation, and coherence, but also of incompatibility, intersection, substitution, exclusion, mutual alteration, displacement, etc. Such an analysis, then, concerns, at a kind of *preconceptual* level, the field in which concepts can coexist and the rules to which this field is subjected. [*AK*, p. 60]

Concepts are no longer referred to an ideality, to the activity of an individual or collective consciousness, but are determined by rules of formation that operate "according to a sort of uniform anonymity, on all individuals who undertake to speak in this discursive field" (*AK*, p. 63). Just as it is no longer possible to consider empirically the concept-contents

74

or ideas of a particular discourse at the enunciative level, it is futile to look for a fundamental project, a metahistorical design that could he held to motivate a discourse. The manner in which discursive transformations take place is attributable to strategic choices that manifest themselves as themes or theories. Such thematic or theoretical choices not only determine the particular conceptual formations that organize a discourse but affect each individual concept as well, since a concept will necessarily undergo modifications as it passes from one discursive constellation to the next. The desire to discover cause-effect mechanisms that might connect a discourse to an identifiable conscious or unconscious is conditioned by an anthropological bias. Archaeologically speaking, strategies that underlie a discursive practice do not reveal an origin that could serve as a truth-referent but are simple options: "These options are not seeds of discourse (in which discourses are determined in advance and prefigured in a quasi-microscopic form); they are regulated ways (and describable as such) of practising the possibilities of discourse" (AK, p. 70). Notions of origin, depth, and unity are no longer sustained by an archaeological perspective because it does not provide a subject to support them. Such an approach does not therefore recognize the conventional discursive unities of book, oeuvre, or genre, but is predicated on the existence of an archive.

The archive, in turn, contributes to disperse the notion of memory. More specifically, it breaks up the complicity between a subject and his consciousness of a past. Discourse, which has traditionally served to provide a history for a subject as well as subjects for history,[3] has also functioned to

3. One of the early misconceptions about Foucault concerned his supposed ahistoric or antihistorical stance. If anything his work is thoroughly historical although, obviously, the past does not exist for him as it does for traditional historicism, nor does history have the transcendental or teleological status that Hegelian and Marxist approaches recognize. A remarkably cogent statement on Foucault's uses of history is to be found in the preface

maintain the illusion of a memory possessing the capacity to relive the past, to retrieve events from an ever-present preteritness. Society has always provided itself with documents to preserve the traces of its history; such historical texts are understood to contain within their memorial depths the riches of ages gone by. Archaeology transforms documents into monuments, into tangible arrangements of perceptible structures, and analyzes the actual configuration of the discourses that constitute an archive: "Instead of seeing, on the great mythical book of history, lines of words that translate in visible characters thoughts that were formed in some other time and place, we have in the density of discursive practices, systems that establish statements as events (with their own conditions and domain of appearance) and things (with their own possibility and field of use)" (*AK*, p. 128). The archive itself does not have a history but is affected by a *"historical a priori"* which imposes "a condition of reality for statements," that is, there are, within a discursive practice, specific constraints and possibilities that oversee the development, emergence, and transformation of discourses. We no longer have truths waiting to be said or meanings waiting to be realized but "a body of anonymous, historical rules, always determined in the time and space that have defined [in] a given period, and for a given social, economic, geographical, or linguistic area, the conditions of operation of the enunciative function" (*AK*, p. 117). The archive then concerns specifically the *énoncé*, "it is that which defines the mode of occurrence of the statement-thing; it is the system of its functioning" (*AK*, p. 129). It does not represent an explanatory or unifying mechanism but is what permits us to view each discourse in its present singularity and at the

---

to Meaghan Morris and Paul Patton, ed., Michel Foucault: *Power, Truth, Strategy* (Sydney: Feral Publications, 1979). See also "Foucault révolutionne l'histoire," the appendix to Paul Veyne, *Comment on écrit l'histoire*, 2d ed. (Paris: Seuil, 1978); and Jonathan Arac, "The Function of Foucault at the Present Time," *Humanities in Society* 3, no. 1 (Winter 1980).

level of the *énoncé*. An archaeological analysis considers discourses "in the *remanence* (*rémanence*) that is proper to them, and which is not that of an ever-realizable reference back to the past event of the formulation" (*AK*, p. 123).

Archaeology does not refer a discourse to a subject but to an archive, to an area that is not the network of circumstances that once witnessed the creation of a discourse and that could therefore help recreate for us that memorable event; it is that specific discursive configuration which permits a discourse to arise, to exist and to function within the framework of social relations and practices, within modes of institutionalized application and cultural usage. Seen from a purely discursive level, neither are *énoncés* produced by nor do they produce a subject; they simply represent us as "this dispersion that we are and make" (*AK*, p. 131). Accordingly, the discourse of Michel Foucault rejects explanations that make use of categories of transcendental purposes or of anthropological justifications. It does not claim a *telos* or a truth, it is neither prophecy nor fulfillment; it establishes itself empirically in the configuration of its archive for which it is both a witness and a participator. In this sense, Foucault's discourse can serve to gauge a major event marking the outlines of the present archive—an event that it helps to identify as the disintegration of the Western logos.

5

The Archaeological Inversion

Although it is aware of its own connections to a certain configuration of the contemporary archive, Foucault's discourse does not pretend to represent the latter or to provide us with a systematic description of its cultural manifestations: "The horizon of archaeology, therefore, is not *a* science, *a* rationality, *a* mentality, *a* culture" (*AK*, p. 159). To a considerable extent, archaeology is a negation of conventional approaches to culture and to the history of thought, and the organization of its specific concerns can occur only by means of a radical reorientation, since it calls for the dissolution of ingrained habits of thought. Foucault's stated intention to "interrogate language not in the direction to which it refers but in the direction that gives it" expresses succinctly the general aim of an archaeological strategy, which is basically a movement away from the Imaginary and toward the Symbolic. The exploration of the Symbolic dimension has to be carried out at the expense of the logos that still holds sway over Western thought; it therefore manifests itself in opposition to established systems of thought—as a strategy to undermine all those approaches and methods that have been valued by a cultural tradition and are set in secure and seemingly natural patterns of thought.

An archaeological approach is subversive by its very situation, by the very nature of the discursive practice in which it is involved; and, in opposing conventional, established intellectual strategies, it provides a perspective that inverts accepted hierarchies and sequences, that disturbs the confidence of time-honored mental categories and rules of cogitation. As the locus of these categories and rules, the subject has been the central element in Foucault's critique. By taking away from the subject his privileges of creation and origin, by denying the subject his status as unifying consciousness, archaeology provides an access to a different reality of discourse. It frees discourse from the conventional metaphors that have always served to make it into an ontological support for the subject and his world. Metaphors expressing depth, continuity, origin, and totality are shown to be nothing more than empty abstract notions once the subject is made to lose his constituent role—the function he enjoys in the Imaginary as the central origin of perception. Discourse is no longer seen as a document that hides within its depths other discourses to be uncovered through interpretation or exegesis; it does not allow anymore for the reconstruction of a continuous process of causes and effects in which it would fit as an organic entity; discourse, in this perspective, cannot restore the unique experience of its origin and, taken as an oeuvre, cannot serve to reconstitute either a sociological or a psychological unity. All such reconstructions are but the projections of a subject that sees himself as the source of perception and for whom discourse serves as the mirror for his own phantasms. By containing and representing "ideas" or "mentalities," a private or public "consciousness" or "unconscious," discourse has served to provide man with an image of himself. Archaeology reveals the self-serving application with which Western man has developed habits of thought that sustain the validity of his discourse while covering up the basically circular process through which his language represents reality. From an archaeological perspective then, the history of Western thought is a history of self-delusion.

At the same time, this perspective provides a corrective—an alternative mode of dealing with discourse and with its historical reality. Such is the purpose accomplished by genealogy (a term Foucault borrows from Nietzsche), an approach he describes as "a form of history which can account for the constitution of knowledges, discourses, domains of objects, etc., without having to make a reference to a subject which is either transcendental in relation to the field of events or runs in its empty sameness throughout the course of history." When an archaeological investigation does concern itself with the subject, it is only "to arrive at an analysis which can account for the constitution of the subject within a historical framework" (*PK*, p. 117). In place of the subject, it is the systematicness of discursive formations that is highlighted, and the main purpose of a genealogy of knowledge is "to reveal the heterogenous systems which, masked by the self, inhibit the formation of any form of identity" (*LCMP*, p. 162). From an archaeological vantage point, the subject, as the Imaginary avatar of the self, is itself no more than a historical product of discourse and can no longer hide the perpetually moving discursive dimension that both founds it and disperses it.

A traditional historical approach aims to eliminate the subject in the name of an ideal of objectivity: "As the demagogue is obliged to invoke truth, laws of essences, and eternal necessity, the historian must invoke objectivity, the accuracy of facts, and the permanence of the past" (*LCMP*, p. 158). Ironically, this attempt to do away with the subject only produces a metaphysics of the subject: the latter is eradicated by a philosophical sleight of hand which also manages, with the same motion, to shut away the accumulated mass of truths, untested assumptions, ethical and aesthetic a prioris that go into the making of this "objectivity." The naïveté of this approach is due to the simplistic commonsensical model that obtains in a conventional philosophy of history, whose error, according to Foucault, "is grammatical; it treats the present as framed by the past and future: the present is a former future where its form was prepared and the past, which will occur in the future, preserves the identity of its content. First, this sense of the present requires a logic of essences (which establishes the present in memory) and of concepts (where the present is established as a knowledge of the future), and then a metaphysics of a crowned and coherent cosmos, of a hierarchical world" (*LCMP*, p. 176). The specific order of the world is enacted and sanctioned by the authority of certain discourses—those discourses that provide, for every society, an "established régime of thought." The major critical thrust of Foucault's archaeology is aimed, then, at "the tyranny of globalizing discourses" and is grounded on a strategy that promises to "emancipate historical knowledges from that subjection, to render them, that is, capable of opposition and of struggle against the coercion of a theoretical, unitary, formal and scientific discourse" (*PK*, p. 85). If scientism and common sense are perceived as the principal constitutive forces of the Western *ratio*, of the intellectual grid that establishes our mental categories and our social and cultural priorities, an appropriate inversion of the existing pattern may be achieved by acategorical thought, by "a theory of thought that is completely freed from both the subject and the object," by a radical supposition: "What if thought freed itself from common sense and decided to function only in its extreme singularity? What if it adopted the disreputable bias of the paradox, instead of complacently accepting its citizenship in the *doxa*?" (*LCMP*, p. 182).

To be sure, such designs are completely at odds with the prevailing mode of rational inquiry and epistemological consciousness, yet they cannot simply be viewed as a negation of the existing rationality. Archaeology does not attempt to replace the present regime with another, "truer" system; it does not aim at revealing existing tautologies, incoherences, and delusions in order to establish a coherence that would serve as a more nearly perfect principle of explanation. For this reason, Foucault's enterprise cannot really be assimilated to traditional strategies by means of a *coincidentia oppositorum,* as the negative analogue of an existing paradigm. Archaeology does not operate dialectically, it does not posit itself as a superior synthesis in an evolution that it supposedly helps to bring about; Foucault therefore refuses to valorize his project: "I adopt the methodical precaution and the radical but unaggressive scepticism which makes it a principle not to regard the point in time where we are now standing as the outcome of a teleological progression which it would be one's business to reconstruct historically: that scepticism regarding ourselves and what we are, our here and now, which prevents one from assuming that what we have is better than—or more than—in the past" (*PK,* p. 49). On the one hand, Foucault's strategy is a conscious intent to avoid the conformation of a history of ideas, which operates in terms of the old and the new, which grants memory an essential status, and which locates itself in a context that it takes to represent the consummation of a historical progression. On the other hand, it does not simply want to be different but focuses on the very gap that produces the difference; archaeology both establishes a discontinuity and dwells on it, making it into "both an instrument and an object of research" (*AK,* p. 9). This is archaeology's way of being true to its archive and, in doing so, it poses the problem of its own existence: an archaeology of knowldge has as its correlative a pervasive self-consciousness, which is due, quite understandably, to the disintegration of a central and sovereign subject. The loss of the subject lets archaeology develop its strategy at a level of investigation that will allow it "to question our will to truth; to restore to discourse its character as an event, to abolish the sovereignty of the signifier" (*DL,* p. 229). While its effect may therefore be subversive, its primary design manifests itself as an intention to invert the given order of thought, to approach discourse not from the side that gives off meaning, but from the direction that organizes its capacity for meaning; it tries to outflank discourse as it were, in the hope of detecting the initial impulses that set it in motion. Consequently, archaeology does not receive discourse as a fully constituted signifying substantiality but attempts to disclose the particular constraints and determinisms that are normally occluded by a conventional apprehension. It problematizes that aspect of discourse which is held to be its inherent, therefore natural function—that of representing a world and of disclosing truths.[1]

Thus, from an archaeological standpoint, the production of knowledge is not a "natural" process. Knowledge does not arise as the spontaneous, inevitable, and beneficial by-product of discursive practice: it is something that is legitimized by certain kinds of discourses, those discourses that enjoy a central and dominating position in a culture, the ones that are valorized as appropriate sources of truth. Foucault perceives the crystallization of such officially sanctioned discourses, as, for example, the sciences, to be a fundamental characteristic of Western discursive practice. It is as if certain amorphous areas that initially appear to constitute a vague, undefinable body of knowledge were capable of undergoing a process of internal organization, enrichment, and

1. It has been remarked that Foucault's strategy is perhaps not able, in spite of its claims, to avoid the phenomenological temptation and that it manifests, after all, a certain "parti pris du plein," a predisposition for plenitude. Although Foucault empties discourse of content, he tends to hypostatize it and one may therefore wonder "what good is it, indeed, to understand words outside of their reference to things (such as the psychological depth of the author or the reader), what good is it to understand them as the absence of things (and of subjectivity), if it is to make them into things once more?" (François Wahl, "Philosophie et structuralisme," in *Qu'est-ce que le structuralisme?* ed. Oswald Ducrot, Tzvetan Todorov, Dan Sperber, Moustafa Safouan, and François Wahl [Paris: Seuil, 1968], pp. 314 and 316). Such a critique loses some of its cogency, however, if we accept archaeology as a means to something else and not as an end in itself—the end being Foucault's genealogical purpose.

maturing, a process that imperceptibly causes an amalgam of discursive raw material to jell into the rigorous and impeccable arrangement of a science. Discourses can thus be seen as the integral parts of relatively independent and proliferous cognitive systems. From Foucault's perspective, the functioning of discourses constitutes a phenomenon which, as Colin Gordon puts it, "consists in the singular emergence in Western thought during the past four centuries of discourses which construct programmes for the formation of a social reality . . . , of discourses whose object (in both senses of the word) is the rendering rationalisable, transparent and programmable of the real" (*PK*, p. 245). The evolution of discourses thus follows a path leading to an eventual and inevitable claim to scientific status and authority. Yet, although it appears inevitable, this peculiar epistemologization of discourses in Western culture is by no means miraculous, and the notable merit of Foucault's approach is its capacity to account for this discursive tendency toward increasing levels of positivity and formalization. Foucault finds that the functioning of scientific discourses is basically ideological and that "the hold of ideology over scientific discourse and the ideological functioning of the sciences . . . are articulated where science is articulated upon knowledge" (*AK*, p. 185). Because it is predicated on a specific image of man, an ideology owes its truth to the occlusion of the historical process that has been instrumental in producing this particular representation of human nature or destiny. The translation of a knowledge into a science is inevitably ideological because it grants an official recognition to certain discourses. It is a move that is intimately linked to the strategies of a political economy and its accomplishment reveals the collusion of knowledge and power.

Even though the notion of power was absent in his earlier works, Foucault has realized retrospectively that discursive relations of power and the conjunction of knowledge and power strategies were implied in some of his initial analyses

(*PK*, p. 115).[2] What he now finds to have been specifically lacking in a book such as *The Order of Things* is the "problem of the 'discursive régime,' of the effects of power peculiar to the play of statements" (*PK*, p. 113). It is the specific level of the *énoncé*, as it is defined in *The Archaeology of Knowledge*, that has allowed Foucault to develop a theory of power. It is a level that marks the emergence of discourses in a sociopolitical context—a level at which discourses can be seen to be constituted by *énoncés*. The latter are perceived as strategic commodities produced, reproduced, distributed, transmitted, appropriated, and transformed in an economy that determines their specific value,

> a value that is not defined by their truth, that is not gauged by the presence of a secret content; but which characterizes their place, their capacity for circulation and exchange, their possibility of transformation, not only in the economy of discourse, but, more generally, in the administration of scarce resources. In this sense, discourse ceases to be what it is for the exegetic attitude: an inexhaustible treasure from which one can always draw new, and always unpredictable riches; a providence that has always spoken in advance, and which enables one to hear, when one knows how to listen, retrospective oracles: it appears as an asset—finite, limited, desirable, useful—that has its own rules of appearance, but also its own conditions of appropriation and operation; an asset that consequently, from the moment of its existence (and not only in its "practical applications"), poses the question of power; an asset that is, by nature, the object of a struggle, a political struggle. [*AK*, p. 120]

From an archaeological perspective, discourse ceases to be the alibi it is in an anthropological or Imaginary mode, in

2. Power is, of course, one of the major themes with which Foucault's work has been identified ever since the publication of *Discipline and Punish*. At his recent speech at USC, however, Foucault pointed out that the goal of his work during the last twenty years "has not been to analyze the phenomenon of power," nor "to elaborate the foundations of such an analysis," but rather to investigate the problematic of the subject.

which it always refers to a place other than where it actually is situated: to the *topos* of man's "real nature" or to a fundamental essence of thought. Archaeology disqualifies ideal themes that function in terms of a teleology or of a transcendental consciousness and uses a language designed to break the hold of traditional models of rationality, in order to reveal a more crucial level of discursive relations. As Foucault explains: "The longer I continue, the more it seems to me that the formation of discourses and the genealogy of knowledge need to be analyzed, not in terms of types of consciousness, modes of perception and forms of ideology, but in terms of tactics and strategies of power" (*PK*, p. 77). It follows therefore, that an analysis of power relations will no longer employ the notions of signifier or content and will not seek to determine the truth or validity of a discourse.

In establishing his archaeological strategy, Foucault has set up, of necessity, a terminological and conceptual framework that refuses, by its very form and design, to accommodate conventional thought. He intends first to avoid all those words "that are already overladen with conditions and consequences," and instead deals, for example, with "discursive objects," analyzing the formation of such objects in terms of institutionalized and codified laws of emergence, delimitation, and specification. Foucault shows them emerging on such "discursive surfaces" as the family, place of work, religious community, or social milieu (*AK*, pp. 38–41). These objects are then seen to undergo a delimitation imposed by the authority of specialized fields such as medicine, jurisprudence, religion, artistic and literary criticism. In the context of these official domains, discursive objects are further subjected to grids of specification that serve to arrange groupings, impose classifications, and allow for the development of a systematic explanatory scheme. This tactic of terminological estrangement not only serves to disrupt traditional models and patterns, but also helps to outline, in a tentative manner that seeks to be suggestive rather than prescriptive, the area of relations and determinants that provides a discourse with a context of power-knowledge strategies.

In place of the traditional and relatively simple three-dimensional model representing discourse as a surface covering a depth and connected in a linear fashion to other surfaces supported by contents, Foucault elaborates a highly complex, multitiered conceptual structure whose purpose is precisely to suggest the inevitably entangled existence of discursive relations. Thus, using the example of the relations that existed in the nineteenth century between the bourgeois family and the judicial system, he distinguishes three levels marking the functional reality of discourse, including "a system of *real* or *primary relations*, a system of *reflexive* or *secondary relations*, and a system of relations that might properly be called *discursive*" (*AK*, p. 45). The primary relations, according to this scheme, are the ones that actually existed. The secondary ones are those that were produced in the discourse of psychiatrists; these relations, however, were actualized in an Imaginary mode, because whatever psychiatrists "could say about the relations between the family and criminality does not reproduce . . . the interplay of real dependencies." Furthermore, the discourse of the psychiatrists is incapable of reproducing "the interplay of relations that make possible and sustain the objects of psychiatric discourse," since these interrelations fall within the area of the Symbolic and are overseen, specifically, by an archive and an *episteme*. The aim of an archaeology, then, is to recognize these different levels of the Real, the Imaginary, and the Symbolic, and, above all, to disclose the specificity of the purely discursive or Symbolic relations in order to reveal "their interplay with the other two kinds."

In addition to these strata of discursive formation, Foucault distinguishes several levels of archaeological analysis from which a discourse can be approached as a unique configuration of events. Thus, there is "the level of the appearance of objects, types of enunciation, concepts, strategic choices (or transformations that affect those that already exist); the level of the derivation of new rules of formation on the basis of rules that are already in operation—but always in the element of a single positivity; lastly, a fourth level, at which the substitution of one discursive formation for another takes place (or the mere appearance and disappearance of a positivity)" (*AK*, p. 171). This latest theoretical display calls for another disclaimer, however, and it is important to note that this imposing, perhaps even overwhelming conceptual apparatus does not pretend to the status of an explanatory model; it will not provide the key for a definitive interpretation but is a heuristic device that questions itself as much as it problematizes the objects of its investigation. If there is a dialectical pattern to be discovered in Foucault's method, then it is perhaps here, in the perpetual give and take between his discourse and the discourses he treats. The interaction produces constant modifications in Foucault's approach and these changes inevitably modify the relation between archaeology and its objects. This relation, however, is by no means antithetical, and while it could be said that archaeology operates in terms of an empirical (but not a transcendental) dialectics, its aim, quite clearly, is never to produce a new synthesis, but rather to postpone indefinitely the very possibility of such a synthesis.

Foucault's interest in what he calls the counter-sciences is revealing in this regard. These are the illegitimate, sometimes popular forms of knowledge that exist alongside the officially recognized bodies of knowledge and have been disqualified by them. The existence of such antisciences is important not so much because they can serve to discredit institutionalized types of knowledge, but because they help to reveal the specific mechanisms that are at work producing truth in a particular culture. And although Foucault finds that "our critical discourses of the last fifteen years have in effect discovered their essential force in this association be-

tween the buried knowledges of erudition and those disqualified from the hierarchy of knowledges and sciences,"
he also recognizes that the critical thrust of his own discourse is "opposed primarily not to the contents, methods
or concepts of a science, but to the effects of the centralizing
powers which are linked to the institution and functioning
of an organized scientific discourse within a society such as
ours" (PK, pp. 82, 84). Foucault's application of archaeological or genealogical strategies disqualifies notions of content,
themes of ideological or psychological unity from their claim
to intellectual domination, and shows that the crucial determinants which establish the privilege of certain discourses
are to be found at the purely discursive level of knowledge-power mechanisms. This approach constitutes the fundamental inversion accomplished by Foucault's critique.
Whereas, traditionally, the value and impact of a discourse
was attributed to something else that either preceded discourse (an ideology, a consciousness), or was contained by
discourse (meaningful riches and secrets), Foucault makes
us see the strategic value of discourse itself. It is no longer
the hollow vehicle whose worth was always to be found
somewhere else, it is a solid, concrete, and self-sufficient
construct that effects dominance and exudes power. The perception of this reality has become possible because considerations of meanings and mentalities have been replaced by a
concern for a very basic mode of human existence; specifically, this perception produces an awareness of the concrete
effect discourses have had and continue to exert on human
bodies.

6

Discourse, Power, Bodies

Taken as an event, as the fulfillment of certain enunciative requirements, a discourse involves much more than the creation and transmission of meaning. It finds itself linked to a field of nondiscursive phenomena as well as to expressed forms of thought. Foucault shows that a discursive object such as "sexuality," for example, is determined by an entire "apparatus," that is by a "thoroughly heterogeneous ensemble consisting of discourses, institutions, architectural forms, regulatory decisions, laws, administrative measures, scientific statements, philosophical, moral and philanthropic propositions, in short, the said as much as the unsaid" (*PK*, p. 194).[1] Hence a study of discursive functions can involve several approaches in the light of which a discourse can be viewed. The latter presents several facets and does not behave in a single unified and purposeful fashion; "thus, a particular discourse can figure at one time as the programme of an institution, and at another it can function as a means of jus-

1. It is interesting to note that, in this interview given in 1977 and published as "Le jeu de Michel Foucault" in *Ornicar* (10 July), Foucault also uses the term "apparatus" as a retrospective explanation of the *episteme* pointing out that "what I should like to do now is to try and show that what I call an apparatus is a much more general case of the *episteme*; or rather, that the *episteme* is a specifically *discursive* apparatus, whereas the apparatus in its general form is both discursive and non-discursive, its elements being much more heterogeneous" (*PK*, p. 197).

tifying or masking a practice which itself remains silent, or as a secondary re-interpretation of this practice, opening out for it a new field of rationality" (*PK*, pp. 194–95). Such an attempt to make clear distinctions among the various levels at which a discourse can be seen to produce its effects is characteristic of the analyses Foucault develops in *Discipline and Punish* and *The History of Sexuality*. These two works are no longer cast in the purely theoretical mold of the two preceding ones, but aim to apply the understanding provided by an archaeological perspective to the development of a different appreciation of certain social, political, and cultural mechanisms at work in Western discursive economies. Specifically, Foucault is concerned with the concrete effects that discourses can have on the physical existence of men, women, and children; his analyses thus purport to reveal those minute yet tenacious holds that a discourse can establish over and around our bodies.

The connections that link a discourse to bodies result from the discourse's capacity to produce and to convey power. In this regard, Foucault distinguishes two basic modes in which discourses have generally operated. One is the meaningful, visible, and official function that is carried out in the context of a logos and according to some privileged models of order and coherence. The sovereign is thus the principal model according to which laws and constitutions are encoded and doctrines of right are imposed. The state and its apparatus, all the major social institutions have developed according to this fundamental principle of sovereignty and "in Western societies since the Middle Ages, the exercise of power has always been formulated in terms of law [*droit*]" (*HS*, p. 87).[2] Political analyses have traditionally been carried out in ac-

2. The translation of the French word *droit* as "law" fails to bring out the connotation of "right" that it also has, and I have therefore found it necessary to indicate the original French term in brackets to suggest this ambiguity. If we take the second meaning into consideration, the subterfuge of power appears even more insidious since the latter is seen to operate under the cover of an inherent "right" rather than the aegis of an arbitrary "law."

cordance with this model of a sovereign right, whose imposition is validated by yet another model—that of contract—which establishes the jurisdiction of a state over the individual members of a society. In this guise, power is seen to derive from above, from a center whence it is gradually diffused to the lowest levels of social stratification and to the most minute elements of the social body. Accordingly, power has usually been understood as a negative force of oppression or repression: there are the subjects who possess power and those subjected to it.

From Foucault's standpoint, what really takes place is quite different. The traditional representation of power actually serves to hide the effective mechanisms of power and covers up those strategies that are the real sources of it. Just as the theme of a subject produces an elision of the enunciative reality of a discourse, that of a sovereign power occludes the networks of power operative in discursive strategies. Foucault therefore finds it necessary to turn the accepted perspective upside down: "My general project over the past few years has been, in essence, to reverse the mode of analysis followed by the entire discourse of right from the time of the Middle Ages. My aim, therefore, was to invert it, to give due weight that is, to the fact of domination, to expose both its latent nature and its brutality" (PK, p. 95). Instead of seeking to delineate "that solid and global kind of domination that one person exercises over others, or one group over another," the kind of domination that is represented at the level where discourses are "meaningful," Foucault observes the action of discourses behind the facade of signifiers and is concerned with "power at its extremities, in its ultimate destinations, with those points where it becomes capillary . . . the point where power surmounts the rules of right which organize and delimit it and extends itself beyond them" (PK, p. 96). This is then the level at which power is organized into effective strategies that take an immediate hold over bodies; it is a dimension in which power operates in a manner that frequently contradicts the meaning given off by the facade of a discourse, going its own way, developing its own purposes, beyond and contrary to anything the discourse may seem to be officially proclaiming.

In order to effectuate the kind of inversion that Foucault proposes, it is also necessary to eliminate other models commonly used to sustain traditional analyses of power. Foucault therefore rejects the standard explanations phrased in terms of "the violence-ideology opposition, the metaphor of property, the model of the contract or of conquest" (DP, p. 28). Contrary to a popular and commonsensical discernment, "power is not something that is acquired, seized or shared, something that one holds on to or allows to slip away" (HS, p. 94). When the opposition violence-ideology is used as an explanatory device, it inevitably brings with it a metaphysics of the subject, since ideology presupposes "a human subject on the lines of the model provided by classical philosophy, endowed with a consciousness which power is then thought to seize on" (PK, p. 58). By eliminating the active and conscious participation of subjects from the most fundamental strategies of power, Foucault is able to develop his own theoretical paradigm for locating the sources and effects of power. Accordingly, he finds that "relations of power are not in a position of exteriority with respect to other types of relationships (economic processes, knowledge relationships, sexual relations), but are immanent in the latter; . . . relations of power are not in superstructural positions, with merely a role of prohibition or accompaniment" (HS, p. 94). Thus, to the familiar prohibitive, oppressive, and violent function of power, Foucault opposes a radically different perception. To the motivation of a selective intentionality, he contraposes a ubiquitous and ever-present strategy of power relations that permeates all levels of social existence. At the same time, he does not deny the reality of domination and oppression and does not dispute the existence of forces that are exerted from above in the name of some sovereign right. His purpose is to show that these are secondary manifestations of power and that this particular kind of domination would be thoroughly ineffective if power relations did not already exist at a lower level, and if a whole network of minute mechanisms actualizing the application of power were not already in place: "Between every point of a social body, between a man and a woman, between the members of a family, between a master and a pupil, between every one who knows and every one who does not, there exist relations of power which are not purely and simply a projection of the sovereign's great power over the individual; they are rather the concrete, changing soil in which the sovereign's power is grounded, the conditions which make it possible for it to function" (*PK*, p. 187). The problem, obviously, is to develop an approach that will allow us to grasp this power that is invisible yet is active everywhere and all the time—all those "myriad effects of power" that underlie its more visible manifestations but can also work at cross-purposes with the stated aims of the apparent strategies.

Foucault realizes that we are still far from having developed any effective approach to such problems and he recognizes the vagueness and insufficiency of his own theorizing. Nevertheless, he considers such an undertaking to be essential and finds there is an urgent need for "an analytics of power that no longer takes law [*droit*] as a model and a code" (*HS*, p. 90), because theories of sovereignty and all the legal codes that derive from them have always served to conceal the actual workings of power. Doctrines of right, contractual principles, may well establish a cohesive social scheme and determine the legal status of each member in it; yet there also exist various systems of coercions that are perhaps even more effective means of constituting the social body and of determining everyone's relationship to this body. And although there is a constant interchange of effects between the two levels—between the official, visible area of power and the subterranean, pervasive, and constantly moving power mechanisms—"they cannot possibly be reduced to each other. The powers of modern society are exercised through, on the basis of, and by virtue of, this very heterogeneity between a public right of sovereignty and a polymorphous disciplinary mechanism" (*PK*, p. 106).

Still, there is the common discursive element necessary for both modes of power; consequently, the starting point for any attempt at defining the various effects of power that underlie its more visible manifestations has to be an analysis of discourse and its functions, since it is clear that the "manifold relations of power which permeate, characterize and constitute the social body . . . cannot themselves be established, consolidated nor implemented without the production, accumulation, circulation and functioning of a discourse" (*PK*, p. 93). Discourse actualizes the multiple strategies of power and oversees their application. The perception of this discursive function is provided by what Foucault terms "an ascending analysis of power," which is an approach going counter to conventional explanations: "In short, it is a question of orienting ourselves to a conception of power which replaces the privilege of the law with the viewpoint of the objective, the privilege of prohibition with the viewpoint of tactical efficacy, the privilege of sovereignty with the analysis of a multiple and mobile field of force relations, wherein far-reaching, but never completely stable, effects of domination are produced" (*HS*, p. 102). Such an approach is obviously compatible with Foucault's archaeological and genealogical strategies, since it rejects the anthropological bias with all its Imaginary representations of law and order and refuses the facile explanations that have recourse to the consciousness of a purposeful and dominating subject, either individual or collective.

The inversion that characterizes Foucault's approach to the whole question of power brings about a corresponding change in the notion of power itself. From a negative force

95

it is turned into a positive and productive effect, into a strategy that supports and reinforces the particular forms of social existence that have evolved in Western cultures since the eighteenth century. This strategy manifests itself particularly in techniques of discipline and normalization, in those "new methods of power whose operation is not ensured by right but by technique, not by law but by normalization, not by punishment but by control, methods that are employed on all levels and in forms that go beyond the state and its apparatus" (HS, p. 89). This new perspective on the function of power provided by Foucault's analysis tends to have a diffusive effect: by associating power with discursive phenomena it avoids the temptation to hypostatize power and disperses whatever substantiality the latter may have inherited from traditional notions. Power no longer appears as something to possess, to apply, to undergo; it is no longer seen as an exterior force surrounding and accompanying certain manifestations of social status or economic advantage. It is an inherent characteristic of all human relations, but since it is intangible, "one needs to be nominalistic, no doubt: power is not an institution, and not a structure; neither is it a certain strength we are endowed with; it is the name that one attributes to a complex strategical situation in a particular society" (HS, p. 93). Paradoxically, it is this very lack of substance that makes power so effective, and Foucault recognizes that "what makes power hold good, what makes it accepted is simply the fact that it doesn't only weigh on us as a force that says no, but that it traverses and produces things, it induces pleasure, forms of knowledge, produces discourse" (PK, p. 119). To be sure, the effects of these invisible yet pervasive manifestations of power are quite real and it is with these effects—discernible at the level where discourses take a hold on bodies and affect the everyday existence of humans—that Foucault is concerned above all.

Two major areas of investigation have provided Foucault

with the concrete elements for outlining an analytics of power; they are the domains of penal theory and practice and of sexuality. *Discipline and Punish,* which Foucault wrote as "a historical background to various studies of the power of normalization and the formation of knowledge in modern society" (*DP,* p. 308), examines an episode in the history of Western penal systems. It is a study of all the characteristic institutions and techniques, the various means and justifications of punishment, that marked the transition from the classical to the modern *episteme* in the West—that went from the grotesquely violent and spectacular executions displaying the power of monarchies to the more uniform and humane use of incarceration typical of modern applications of justice. Of course, to assert that in the context of penal codes discourse has a definite effect on bodies may seem like an obvious, and therefore trivial, observation. Yet, as Foucault demonstrates, these effects can be surprisingly ubiquitous and subtle, and the imposition of discipline and punishment is accompanied by a whole dimension of unstated assumptions, of unsuspected consequences, of ethical and epistemological issues that are veiled from public view by the unquestionable authority of ideological guarantees.

It is worth noting first that the power fostered by penal systems is not of a special or unusual variety but is only a more revealing manifestation of power in general and—like all other forms of power—it is cognitively motivated. The fundamental thesis of Foucault's work on penal theory and practice posits the existence of intimate and powerful bonds between economies of punishment and official fields of knowledge. This inevitable connection between knowledge and power is axiomatic for Foucault: "The exercise of power perpetually creates knowledge and, conversely, knowledge constantly induces effects of power" (*PK,* p. 52). Recognized forms of knowledge always bring power, and power in turn justifies the formation of specific kinds of knowledge. The subjects that know and the subjects or objects to be known are all integral elements of power-knowledge strategies and are determined by the historical evolution of these networks. Consequently, it is this particular collusion—the mutual support that the exercise of power and the development of knowledge provide for each other—which endows discourses with the capacity to establish a hold on bodies. Specifically, this strategy consists of providing the body with a soul, with an abstract principle in the name of which the body can then be treated, manipulated, molded; and, although it is quite real, "this real, non-corporal soul is not a substance; it is the element in which are articulated the effects of a certain type of power and the reference of a certain type of knowledge, the machinery by which the power relations give rise to a possible corpus of knowledge, and knowledge extends and reinforces the effects of this power" (*DP*, p. 29). Such a mechanism constitutes the fundamental difference between the single-minded violence of classical techniques, according to which the body was a thing of the sovereign, and the more humane types of punishment that have been developed since the eighteenth century.

This general humanization of penal methods, according to Foucault, has been the result of an "epistemologico-juridical" process that has had the effect of making "the technology of power the very principle both of the humanization of the penal system and of the knowledge of man" (*DP*, p. 23). The practice of punishment is therefore accompanied by a vast apparatus of techniques, knowledges, and scientific discourses: these are the discourses that make the body available for subjection by rendering it amenable to control and correction. It is no longer criminality as such that is being treated but the criminal; and Foucault observes that the individual law-breaker is considered not so much in terms of a general discourse on crime as in the context of a certain "political economy" of the body, of certain processes of objectification that bring an individual into the realm of a "political technology of the body." As a result, it becomes necessary to consider the systems of power operative in society in general since these new techniques and procedures of control and subjection quickly overflowed the boundaries of the penal domain and penetrated all forms of socialization.

The development of Western civilization has thus been accompanied by the parallel evolution of an "art of the human body," and punishment has been only one of several purposes for which this art has been found useful. The phenomenon of the "disciplines" constitutes the most pervasive application of this art, of this new "mechanics of power." An investigation of what Foucault describes as a "political anatomy" lets us appreciate "how one may have a hold over others' bodies, not only so that they may do what one wishes, but so that they may operate as one wishes, with the techniques, the speed and the efficiency that one determines. Thus discipline produces subjected and practised bodies, 'docile' bodies. Discipline increases the forces of the body (in economic terms of utility) and diminishes these same forces (in political terms of obedience)" (*DP*, p. 138). The new techniques that make up the disciplines provide the necessary cohesion for an effective social organization in which it is specifically the bodies that acquire a political significance, because each body must be made to fit into a general scheme of economic utilization: "its constitution as labor power is possible only if it is caught up in a system of subjection (in which need is also a political instrument meticulously prepared, calculated and used)" (*DP*, p. 26). The capitalistic scheme of civilization thus seeks to maximize the use of every body by programming its needs in terms of consumption and by monitoring its efficiency in terms of production. Consumption and production are the two poles around which the development of power-knowledge strategies will necessarily gravitate.

The rise of capitalism has brought with it the need to reconcile economic processes with demographic and biological factors, since the individual members of a capitalistic society must be integrated as efficiently as possible into a design predicated on the accumulation of capital and the circulation of goods. The disciplines, which have made it possible to replace the old principle of "levying-violence" with that of "mildness-production-profit," are thus to be considered "the techniques that make it possible to adjust the multiplicity of men and the multiplication of the apparatuses of production (and this means not only 'production' in the strict sense, but also the production of knowledge and skills in the school, the production of health in the hospitals, the production of destructive force in the army)" (DP, p. 219). Finding the function of these disciplines to be an instrumental, even fundamental factor in the constitution of Western socioeconomic systems, Foucault develops a highly detailed analysis of what constitutes "the political technology of the body." All the methods and techniques making up disciplinary regimes have produced a capacity for control and surveillance thanks to which "the 'physics' of power, the hold over the body, operate according to the laws of optics and mechanics, according to a whole play of spaces, lines, screens, beams, degrees, and without recourse, in principle at least, to excess, force or violence" (DP, p. 177). In accordance with this art of maximizing the socioeconomic integration of individuals, bodies are submitted to sophisticated arrangements of space, they are situated within functional grids that establish order and rank within institutional hierarchies. They are also subjected to a precise temporal syntax that promotes their utility in terms of schedules, elaborate programs that monitor each gesture with regard to a particular task to be performed. Architecture plays a most important role in this context, and the spacial configuration of places that train, correct, discipline, or utilize bodies for productive purposes has become a significant element in these processes of subjection. The panoptic arrangement represents the ultimate scheme in this regard, since it permits a maximum of control with a minimum of surveillance. Indeed, the panopticon holds the promise of the ideal organization, of a society envisioned by the inventor of the panoptic system, Bentham, who "dreamt of transforming [it] into a network of mechanisms that would be everywhere and always alert, running through society without interruption in space or in time. The panoptic arrangement provides the formula for this generalization. It programs, at the level of an elementary and easily transferable mechanism, the basic functioning of a society penetrated through and through with disciplinary mechanisms" (*DP*, p. 209). Foucault has shown that in some ways such an ideal has indeed been pursued by all those strategies that have attempted to control and channel sexuality and that have evolved together with a biopolitical technology of life and desire.

The entire dimension of socioeconomic programming regulated by the disciplines makes up the unspoken counterpart, as it were, of the official representations of social reality. In the framework of what Foucault calls the modern era, that is, approximately the last two centuries, it is evident that "the general juridical form that guaranteed a system of rights that were egalitarian in principle was supported by these tiny, everyday, physical mechanisms, by all those systems of micro-power that are essentially non-egalitarian and asymmetrical that we call the disciplines" (*DP*, p. 222). At first sight, these two forms of social reality also seem to represent two different manifestations of power. It turns out, however, that they not only coexist quite well but actually reinforce each other. This paradox does not therefore constitute a contradiction from the point of view of an effective social arrangement, and Foucault points out that the ultimate purpose of panopticism, for example, is "to make the effective mechanisms of power function in opposition to the formal framework that it had acquired" (*DP*, p. 222). Both levels of discursive practice—the intended "ideological" effect with its rhetoric of egalitarianism and libertarianism, and the accompanying deployment of micro-powers, of coercive manipulations—are united in a single purpose, which is to enhance the efficiency of the entire social system, the purpose, in short, of the dominating capitalistic or socialistic ideology. What makes this collusion possible is the epistemological framework within which these two strategies are simultaneously being carried out, a context that is given by the so-called human sciences, those fields of knowledge that have provided the reality of a soul for each individual, but have also justified the subjection of every individual to ever-present transcendent norms.

7

The Truth of the Norm and
the Norm of Truth

The human sciences, which have been instrumental in setting up specific models of behavior and social organization, are characterized, we have seen, by a basically circular epistemological pattern already highlighted in *The Order of Things*. They have functioned to determine a certain truth of man by creating an image of his humanity; however, they have been bound to an analytic of finitude that leads them to posit their truths on the basis of their own inherent limitations. Truth in this regard has not set man free but has instituted subjection, since "the man described for us, whom we are invited to free, is already himself the effect of a subjection much more profound than himself. A 'soul' inhabits him and brings him to existence, which is itself a factor in the mastery that power exercises over the body. The soul is the effect and instrument of a political anatomy; the soul is the prison of the body" (*DP*, p. 30). This effect of scientifically oriented humanistic discourses is particularly evident in modern penal systems, whose institution is predicated on a "humanization" but whose function is to define the limits of both the law and humanity: "Humanity in the sentences was the rule given to a system of punishment that must fix their limits on both. The 'man' that must be respected in the sentence was the juridical and moral form given to this double delimitation" (*DP*, p. 89). As we saw in the preceding chapter, Foucault's analyses effectively bring out the dual functioning of discourses which, on the one hand, socialize bodies by making them tame and amenable to the effects of the second purpose—which is the definition and organization of the restraints and coercions to be applied. What is noteworthy in this process is the relation the two discursive effects maintain with each other, whereby one serves to hide the activity of the other. Such a strategy is not intentionally deceptive but is required by the very nature of power, whose success "is proportional to its ability to hide its own mechanisms" (HS, p. 86). The interaction of the two modes of discursive agency is successful to the extent that it manages to conceal the basically disinterested and contingent nature of its operations. This basic process of socialization does not require an a priori subjectivity to be effective, it is always already in effect.

Obviously, there are also certain interests that seek to profit from this process by subsuming it under the overriding authority of certain truths. This is accomplished through an appeal to a reason capable of disclosing truths by virtue of its disinterested and "objective" nature. At the same time, such discourses of truth are neither interested in nor capable of taking into consideration the Symbolic dimension of discursive activity within which they are integrated. Consequently, in order to accomplish their aims, they must inevitably rely on strategies of domination and oppression. For Foucault, truth is eminently political by nature and participates, by definition, in power-knowledge strategies. In his ongoing series of works devoted to the history of sexuality, he proposes to undertake an analysis of truth from precisely such a perspective. He intends to "constitute the 'political economy' of a will to knowledge" (HS, p. 73) in order to reveal the role that sexuality has played in the elaboration of pervasive power-truth strategies in Western culture. This undertaking derives from the discovery that sex has been placed "at the center of a formidable *petition to know.*" This obligation to know about sex, which was imposed several centuries ago, represents in fact "a double petition, in that we are compelled to know how things are with it, while it is suspected of knowing how things are with us" (*HS*, pp. 77–78). Discourses on sexuality, together with those on punishment and disciplines, deal with the physical existence of men, women, and children and prepare the ground for networks of power that can be seen to function in terms of two characteristic modes. In the case of the disciplines, the role of discourse has been to realize the integration of bodies within practical and effective systems of control: "All this was ensured by the procedures of power that characterized the *disciplines*: an *anatomo-politics of the human body*." The second mode in which human life becomes an object of discourse involves biological processes; these include questions of health, procreation, birth, death, and longevity, all the essential aspects of human existence, which thus become the objects of "an entire series of interventions and *regulatory controls: a bio-politics of the population*" (*HS*, p. 139). Bodies are valorized according to an economics of usefulness and of truth, and, in a culture where the effects of power are aimed at life, the fact and act of existence become the objects of a politics of normalization. The management and utilization of bodies are strategies carried out behind the mask of certain "forms that made an essentially normalizing power acceptable" (*HS*, p. 144). These are the constitutions and the codes of morality, the dogmas of political and ethical behavior without which an effective technology of power would not be likely to obtain.

The population becomes in effect a moral subject, and the purpose of ideological discourses, whether they deal with life or with work, is to prepare and organize the individual members of society into subjects on whom power can take hold. With regard to the scientifico-legal complex of knowledges that Foucault examines in *Discipline and Punish*, a body is to be considered as "the property of society, the object of a collective and useful appropriation" (*DP*, p. 109). In the bio-political realm, sex is the element instrumental in the social appropriation of bodies and "the political significance of the problem of sex is due to the fact that sex is located at the point of intersection of the discipline of the body and the control of the population" (*PK*, p. 125). Although this whole question of sex seems at first to derive from practical considerations concerning the physical existence of bodies, it inevitably acquired metaphysical proportions the moment "the project of a science of the subject [began to gravitate], in ever narrowing circles, around the question of sex. Causality in the subject, the unconscious of the subject, the truth of the subject in the other who knows, the knowledge he holds unbeknown to him, all this found an opportunity to deploy itself in the discourse of sex" (*HS*, p. 70). Bodies thus are made into moral subjects, since their reality is in certain significant ways constituted by discourses that provide their truth, a truth that speaks to their physical existence but also works to integrate them into a network of both political and moral anthropological paradigms of knowledge. The subject is constituted so that he may fit into the normal patterns established by society or, in the event of a failure to conform, so that any deviance from the norm might be accurately ascertained.

It is this process of normalization which permits the formation of individuality; however, in the context of power— as Foucault points out—it is a process that is actualized in a "descending" manner: since normalization occurs when the system succeeds in establishing its power at the expense of that of the individual, the less power one has, the more one tends to be individualized. Although in the Middle Ages, or even during the classical era, the most powerful tended to be singled out as subjects of respect, of emulation, of knowledge,

> in a system of discipline, the child is more individualized than the adult, the patient more than the healthy man, the madman

and the delinquent more than the normal and the non-delinquent. In each case, it is towards the first of these pairs that all the individualizing mechanisms are turned in our civilization; and when one wishes to individualize the healthy, normal and law-abiding adult, it is always by asking him how much of the child he has in him, what secret madness lies within him, what fundamental crime he has dreamt of committing.   [*DP*, p. 193]

The individualized subject of modern society is constantly held accountable to the system of the norm—but he must first be made aware of his particular situation: he must realize it and admit it. The technique of the confession has therefore been the most effective tool of social control in both the Christian and the secular legal traditions. Because "the confession is a ritual of discourse in which the speaking subject is also the subject of the statement" (*HS*, p. 61), it leads the individual to recognize himself in the framework of his submission to the appropriate moral or judicial code. By confessing, he establishes an unbreakable bond between himself as subject of the enunciation and his statement; he recognizes both the validity of the system and the fact of his own situation, thus accepting his deviance as an objective truth.[1] The confession is one of those rituals that enhance the social reality within which individuality is formed. In light of Foucault's analyses, it is also one that manifests in a particularly vivid manner the powerful hold that discourses establish over lives, a hold that is not imagined but quite real, since "in fact, power produces; it produces reality; it produces domains of objects and rituals of truth. The individual and the knowledge that may be gained of him belong to this production" (*DP*, p. 194). The individual is thus a product of all the systems of power that function to determine the social purposes of the body, that set up the discourses outlining his truth.

The institutionalization of certain discourses serves to es-

1. Techniques of moral self-examination and the methods of "spiritual direction" that have evolved together with Christianity in the West are some of the subjects that Foucault is currently investigating.

tablish the norms according to which the truth of individuals will be determined, and it is in particular the development of the "sciences of man" that has favored the dual mode in which power can be seen to function in Western societies: "These sciences, which have so delighted our 'humanity' for over a century, have their technical matrix in the petty, malicious minutiae of the disciplines and their investigations" (*DP*, p. 226). Foucault sees little glory in the establishment and rise of these punctilious methods of examination, observation, description, and prescription and their techniques of control and behavior modification. What is important to note is that "from such trifles, no doubt, the man of modern humanism was born" (*DP*, p. 141); it is a humanism still very much involved in an economy of discursive and non-discursive practices, an arrangement that supports strategies of cultural integration and of socioeconomic selection and promotion.

Modern humanism is a system of truths that function to establish norms. We have already seen in the case of penal codes how the discourses that establish the truth of modern man impose their jurisdiction in the name of a sovereign right; they hold it up as an ideal and seem to exert power from above, in its name. Behind these appearances, however, there operates a reverse strategy, which is a productive rather than a repressive force. Foucault finds this pattern to be characteristic of the realm of sexuality as well and observes that "'sexuality' is far more a positive product of power than power was ever repression of sexuality" (*PK*, p. 120). Beneath the discourses on humanity, behind this official representation of our civilization, can be detected an unobtrusive yet untiring activity of forces whose effect is to shape individuals according to the pervasive agency of socioeconomic effects:

> Under the surface of images, one invests bodies in depth; behind the great abstraction of exchange, there continues the

meticulous, concrete training of useful forces; the circuits of communication are the supports of an accumulation and a centralization of knowledge; the play of signs defines the anchorages of power; it is not that the beautiful totality of the individual is amputated, repressed, altered by our social order, it is rather that the individual is carefully fabricated in it, according to a whole technique of forces and bodies. [*DP*, p. 217][2]

It is understandable "why the West has insisted for so long in seeing the power it exercises as juridical and negative rather than as technical and positive" (*PK*, p. 121). The secrecy of the basic mechanism is the necessary condition for the effective functioning of the entire structure, because "power is tolerable only on condition that it mask a substantial part of itself. . . . For it, secrecy is not in the nature of an abuse; it is indispensable to its operation" (*HS*, p. 86). The same kind of necessity governs the creation of individuality, the making of subjects. Since "individuals are the vehicles of power, not its points of application" (*PK*, p. 98), the general impression that holds them to be the butt of power only serves to conceal their active involvement in some strategy for which they are the elements of its articulation.

Those forms of power that openly manifest themselves as modes of repression and domination are thus to be considered in the framework of a positive system of forces. This realization leads Foucault to observe a "functional inversion of the disciplines," which, instead of serving to oppress, "were being asked to play a positive role . . . to increase the possible utility of individuals" (*DP*, p. 210). This productive role that disciplines play in the formation of economic-political systems makes them partake of a new type of power, one that "has been a fundamental instrument in the constitution of industrial capitalism and of the type of society

2. Instead of the phrase "one invests bodies" which implies some responsible agency represented by "one," I think that "bodies are invested" would be a more accurate rendition of the passive French "on" construction. Sheridan's translation in this instance fails to suggest the anonymous nature of power-knowledge strategies, an aspect to which this passage clearly alludes.

that is its accompaniment" (*PK*, p. 105). In a similar fashion, Foucault rejects the theme of sexual repression as a valid explanatory principle and reveals the real source of power implicit in the discourse on sexuality to be an imperative that has functioned as a relentless injunction for Western man: "Not only will you confess to acts contravening the law, but you will seek to transform your desire, your every desire, into discourse" (*HS*, p. 21). The discourse on sexuality has thus exerted a considerable influence on desire itself, intensifying it, modifying it, reorienting it. What has passed for a production of truth has actually been instrumental in producing power, and it is this surreptitious collusion between truth and power that accounts for the force of the latter. Power would indeed be most ineffective if it had only the capacity to repress; "if, on the contrary, power is strong this is because, as we are beginning to realize, it produces effects at the level of desire—and also at the level of knowledge" (*PK*, p. 59). Power has thus the capacity to produce truth, the truth of subjects, and, in effect, the subjects themselves.

Yet, power itself is not produced by a subject or subjects. Only the facade of a sovereign discourse presents itself as the locus of a power that derives from a dominating subject. While power-knowledge strategies are inherent in the cultural practices of a society, they cannot be attributed to a specific origin or endowed with set determinants: they operate in a homeostatic field of forces within which the achievement of stability does not require the original impetus of a conscious purpose. It is not possible therefore to identify effects of power according to a scheme that distinguishes those possessing and applying power from those submitting to it; there is no such thing as "a massive and primal condition of domination, a binary structure with 'dominators' on one side and 'dominated' on the other." Rather, Foucault would have us conceive of "a multiform production of relations of domination which are partially susceptible of integration into overall strategies" (*PK*, p. 142). Any apparent sources of power identifiable with a group or an individual are to be considered as tactics that "were invented and organized from the starting points of local conditions and particular needs" (*PK*, p. 159); as such, they are still to be understood in terms of a strategic field encompassing them. With regard to this larger configuration of power, Foucault tells us not to look for "the headquarters that presides over its rationality." Explanations that put forth causes, purposeful designs, or conspiracies, are obviously Imaginary in their approach and fail to take into account the basically disinterested aspect of power-knowledge systems, a Symbolic aspect that is the "implicit characteristic of the great anonymous, almost unspoken strategies which coordinate the loquacious tactics whose 'inventors' or decisionmakers are often without hypocrisy" (*HS*, p. 95). Without hypocrisy because it is humanly impossible to comprehend, and thus to control, the totality of the process through which power-knowledge systems take effect.

The significant determinants operating through these strategies are to be traced back to the circumstances surrounding the formation of power-knowledge designs. Thus, for example, the coercive techniques of the disciplines did not come to be as a result of concerted planning but because "the economic changes of the eighteenth century made it necessary to ensure the circulation of effects of power through progressively finer channels, gaining access to individuals themselves, to their bodies, their gestures and all their daily actions" (*PK*, pp. 151–52). Likewise, sexuality acquired a political importance in the nineteenth century because "for the first time in history, no doubt, biological existence was reflected in political existence; the fact of living was no longer an inaccessible substrate that only emerged from time to time, amid the randomness of death and its fatality; part of it passed into knowledge's field of control and power's sphere of intervention" (*HS*, p. 142). Sex, as a result, becomes a political object since it not only represents an essential aspect of individual lives but also has a bearing on the existence of the entire species. Simultaneously with this newly acquired significance of sex, there develops a particular strain of knowledge-power that Foucault terms "biopower," which constitutes a strategy intent on developing new truths about mankind and imposing its norms for the effective management of life. Sex, in effect, becomes a basic element in a "political technology of life," in a configuration of forces and effects that develops its own strategies of investigation, control, and domination, according to the needs of its own ecology.

It does not follow, however, from everything that precedes, that real domination does not exist or that there is not, in every society, a particular group or specific individuals taking advantage of existing conditions at the expense of the other members. Although society is indeed "a machine in which everyone is caught, those who exercise power just as much as those over whom it is exercised" (*PK*, p. 156), although no one owns nor controls this machinery, its mechanisms are sure to benefit a certain segment of the population. What Foucault's approach reveals is that domination arises from a particular set of circumstances and is an advantage appropriated by a certain group as a process of socialization develops. With regard to this process, the individuals benefiting from it do not constitute an a priori entity, one that has created the conditions appropriate for domination or one that can be identified by its conspiratorial or "arrivistic" designs: "For a class to become a dominant class, for it to ensure its domination and for that domination to reproduce itself is certainly the effect of a number of actual pre-meditated tactics operating within the grand strategies that ensure this domination. But between the strategy which fixes, reproduces, multiplies and accentuates existing relations of forces, and the class which thereby finds itself in a ruling position, there is a reciprocal relation of production"

(*PK*, p. 203). In a sense then, the class is as much a product of its strategy as the strategy is an inherent part of the class that finds itself in a position to dominate and exploit. This relation of class to strategy is precisely that of subject to discourse: the subject derives its reality from the discourse it enunciates just as a class is defined by the tactics in which it engages.

From an archaeological standpoint, a meaningful enunciation can take place only when a number of conditions have been fulfilled—those conditions that make up the "referential" of the statement, among which the subjective function is of primary importance (*AK*, pp. 91–92). By proffering a discourse, the subject reacts to a set of circumstances that determine his discursive activity. Similarly, the tactics of a social group represent an interaction with a given set of historically determined cultural, economic, and other circumstances. The group produces a discursive apparatus "which has as its major function at a given historical moment that of responding to an *urgent need*. The apparatus thus has a dominant strategic function" (*PK*, p. 195). Therefore, while Foucault is not concerned with seeking or reinterpreting "meanings," he does not deny the existence of meaning for historical subjects; he finds that "the history which bears and determines us has the form of a war rather than that of a language: relations of power, not relations of meaning. History has no 'meaning,' though this is not to say that it is absurd or incoherent. On the contrary, it is intelligible and should be susceptible of analysis down to the smallest detail—but this in accordance with the intelligibility of struggles and tactics" (*PK*, p. 114). It is this sort of intelligibility, normally obscured or covered up by meanings, that allows for an apprehension of knowledge-power effects.

However, struggles, strategies, and tactics do not become intelligible simply because we have understood the manner in which certain truths have been produced and received in a given age: it is also necessary that we appreciate the effect these truths have had and perhaps continue to have on a basic physical existence of the individuals in question. Western intellectual tradition has disconnected consciousness from bodies and it is time to apprehend the humanity of man as something more than a cultural representation; therefore, in carrying out his project, Foucault does not envisage "a 'history of mentalities' that would take account of bodies only through the manner in which they have been perceived and given meaning and value; but a 'history of bodies' and the manner in which what is most material and most vital in them has been invested" (HS, p. 152). As the official representatives of a culture, the discourses that are aimed at modeling and forming proper consciousnesses fail to provide an access to the essential level at which power unfolds its strategies. Since power does not belong to the realm of ideality but manifests itself as a material, physical, corporal effect, it needs to be situated in a dimension of our social existence that has escaped the attention of conventional intellectual approaches:

> What I want to show is how power relations can materially penetrate the body in depth, without depending even on the mediation of the subject's own representations. If power takes hold on the body, this isn't through its having first to be interiorized in people's consciousnesses. There is a network or circuit of bio-power, or somato power, which acts as the formative matrix of sexuality itself, as the historical and cultural phenomenon within which we seem at once to recognize and lose ourselves. [PK, p. 186]

We are caught, then, in an inescapable contradiction with regard to this power that discourse ferries; this particular by-product of discourse is something that profoundly affects our existence, yet it is also an effect that draws upon our existence for its own reality. However, it is this very ambiguity which allows Foucault to reconsider the question of discourse, of man, of man's situation with regard to discourse. Although our existence is a philosophical problem that can be raised within the dimension of discourse, it still very much exceeds the limits of discourse. Consequently, since power partakes of the realm of discourse and of life, an adequate treatment of the question of power requires that we alter our perception of man as a social being, that we reconsider his political status. Thus, if we look behind his cultural facade, man becomes a biological entity, a member of the human species: "If the question of man was raised— insofar as he was a specific living being, and specifically related to other living beings—the reason for this is to be sought in the new mode of relation between history and life: in this dual position of life that placed it at the same time outside history, in its biological environment, and inside human historicity, penetrated by the latter's techniques of knowledge and power" (*HS*, p. 143). An obvious shift in emphasis occurs thus in Foucault's approach since, in addition to the determinisms deriving from an *episteme*, Foucault seems to allow for the indeterminate effects of vitalistic forces. Consequently, his discourse situates itself at the intersection of two modes of self-consciousness: the awareness of his own archive and a consciousness of the extra-discursive dimension that is life itself. In a sense then, discourse is trivial but at the same time it is our most important resource since it holds out the promise of an access to our reality; discourse is, in effect, our destiny because "in the end, we are judged, condemned, classified, determined in our undertakings, destined to a certain mode of living or dying, as a function of the true discourses which are the bearers of the specific effects of power" (*PK*, p. 94). The function of intellect thus needs to be reconciled with a radically altered perception of discourse: the latter is no longer to be considered as "simply discourse," since it brings up the whole question of our human existence. The next two chapters will attempt to ascertain the ways in which the approaches that Foucault develops to these problems modify conventional perceptions of the role and obligations of intellect.

8

The Function of Intellect

Although Foucault's work manifests an implicit injunction against any attempt to write about the author, Foucault is himself acutely aware of his subjectivity, of his particular position with regard to the object of his activity. Thus the function that he assumes as a subject in his own discourse is in a dialectical relation to his own writing: as his discourse develops a genealogy of the discourses it takes for its objects, it raises also the question of its own truth. It does not, however, raise this question in order to resolve it, but rather to maintain it in a permanent state of irresolution. The constant tension between the Imaginary and the Symbolic that his writing produces is usually maintained with the aim of avoiding Imaginary closures and of preserving the Symbolic opening toward the beyond, the outside of discourse. Such an intellectual strategy can be considered an alternative to the traditional approaches that Foucault has worked to discredit. On the other hand, this strategy can also be viewed as an idiosyncrasy whose principal function would be to sustain the credibility of Foucault's discourse. Or, it can be argued that nothing much has occurred after all and whatever Foucault has to offer is just more of the same—in a clever disguise. Is his discourse prophetic, cynical, chimerical, or simply academic? These are some alternatives to consider.

Obviously, one of the great problems that a critical discourse such as Foucault's has to contend with is the problem of language: in carrying out its attacks on certain forms of culture it is inevitably restricted to the expressions, forms, and modalities it has inherited from that same culture. Foucault's writing thus tends to function in a predominantly Imaginary mode whenever his discourse seems to claim its own truth while failing to consider its ethical or political *non dit*. This inclination to ignore its own archaeological determinants and to identify with certain Imaginary themes becomes apparent when, for example, the question of a bourgeois-proletarian struggle is raised. The discussion then occasionally slips into considerations of a scheming intentionality that gives the "bourgeoisie" the substance of an ontological reality: "The bourgeoisie is perfectly well aware that a new constitution or legislature will not suffice to assure its hegemony; it realizes that it has to invent a new technology ensuring the irrigation by effects of power of the whole social body down to its smallest particles. And it is by such means that the bourgeoisie not only made a revolution but succeeded in establishing a social hegemony which it has never relinquished" (*PK*, p. 156). In a similar fashion, the proletariat is sometimes granted the Imaginary existence of a social entity struggling according to the traditional teleological paradigm: "When the proletariat takes power, it may be quite possible that the proletariat will exert towards the classes over which it has just triumphed, a violent, dictatorial and even bloody power."[1] But such forays into the Imaginary are generally short-lived and the substance that an occasional concept acquires quickly dissolves as Foucault's discourse brings into consideration the ecology of relevant power-strategies. Accordingly, the scheming of the bourgeoisie is seen

1. Fons Elders, *Reflexive Water* (London: Souvenir Press, 1974), p. 182. This rather unusual book contains a series of debates organized and conducted on television by Fons Elders, a Dutch professor of philosophy. Foucault takes part in a debate with Noam Chomsky; their subject is "Human Nature: Justice versus Power."

to take place in the context of a particular arrangement of social forces, of economic relations; this pattern establishes domains of privilege and of dependency that can be entered or appropriated by subjects who are not innately destined to the position they eventually acquire.

The power of the bourgeoisie is determined neither genetically nor discursively but by a process that is inherent in the very nature of this power, which is "self-amplifying, in a mode not of conservation but of successive transformations. Hence the fact that its form isn't given in a definitive historical figure as is that of feudalism. Hence both its precariousness and its supple inventiveness" (*PK*, p. 160). In a like manner, the proletariat is not a group already constituted beforehand but represents an area in a social configuration of forces and effects that absorbs the alienated, the marginal, the excluded. This realm of the lowly, the ignoble, and the hapless not only includes identifiable groups such as "women, prisoners, conscripted soldiers, hospital patients, and homosexuals" (*LCMP*, p. 216), but also, in the final analysis may admit anyone at all, because the potential for alienation, marginality, and exclusion exists in everyone: "There is certainly no such thing as 'the' plebs; rather there is, as it were, a certain plebeian quality or aspect (*'de la' plèbe*). There is plebs in bodies, in souls, in individuals, in the proletariat, in the bourgeoisie, but everywhere in a diversity of forms and extensions, of energies and irreducibilities. This measure of plebs is not so much what stands outside relations of power as their limit, their underside, their counter-stroke, that which responds to every advance of power by a movement of disengagement" (*PK*, p. 138). In the particular arrangement of power-knowledge strategies and economic effects that characterizes the capitalistic system, just as there are those who have installed themselves in positions of domination and exploitation, there have to be those who submit, those who, by choice or by chance, find themselves devoid of privileges and who therefore can subsist only marginally.

At the other end of the power scale, there is the propensity for oppression and exploitation: an area supporting more or less violent forms of domination. It is also a domain that is established by discourses; it requires neither a pedigree nor the mark of a social or genetic predestination, and it can be entered by anyone. The subject occupying such an area will model his behavior accordingly—not because of some inborn inclination but because he has assumed a very specific strategic position in a network of discursive and nondiscursive practices.

Such an understanding clearly calls for a revision of the usual approaches to questions of social stratification and political distinction. The familiar methods of Imaginary identification that set up models for classifying consciousnesses and for recognizing homogeneous groups are no longer admissible. Consequently, instead of placing over society the grid that delimits areas of proletariat, bourgeois, or fascist behavior, Foucault applies it to configurations of discursive strategies. Because the individual is a vehicle for power and is open to the various effects produced by the discourses in which he is inextricably enmeshed, he may partake of any of the diverse aspects of social struggles. When asked about the identity of those who oppose each other in a society, Foucault has responded with the following hypothesis: "I would say it's all against all. There aren't immediately given subjects of the struggle, one the proletariat, the other the bourgeoisie. Who fights against whom? We all fight each other. And there is always within each of us something that fights something else" (*PK,* p. 208). Though still vague, the explanation that Foucault provides for social conflicts avoids the facile identifications and comfortable generalizations in which some established theoretical systems have demarcated the limits of good and evil, of progressive and reactionary forces, of friendly and enemy territories.

In the light of Foucault's analyses, it is clear that traditional modes of intellectual activity have become inadequate for dealing with the reality of man's social existence. In the first place, some of these approaches have ignored the fact that "the essence of our life consists, after all, of the political functioning of the society in which we find ourselves."[2] But it is also not enough to recognize this reality and then use it as an alibi or an evasion: to say that everything is political does not reveal a superior vision and does not allow one to evade the real problems by diverting an analysis of existing conditions to one of philosophical or humanistic themes: "Such an analysis must not be telescoped by laying everything at the door of individual responsibility, as was done above all a decade or two ago by the existentialism of self-flagellation . . . it must not be evaded by those displacements that are glibly practiced today: everything derives from the market economy, or from capitalist exploitation, or simply from the rottenness of our society" (PK, p. 189). Furthermore, "the affirmation, pure and simple, of a 'struggle' can't act as the beginning and end of all explanations in the analysis of power-relations" (PK, p. 164), because more frequently than not such an affirmation involves the analyst in a complicity with existing systems of power. It is the analysis of the conditions that make the struggle both possible and necessary, and not the participation in the struggle, that offers a way of escaping the patterns of power-knowledge mechanisms already in place; thus "the problem is not so much that of defining a political 'position' (which is to choose from a pre-existing set of possibilities) but to imagine and to bring into being new schemas of politicization" (PK, p. 190). A different kind of strategy, an "analytic of relations of power" has to be developed to make possible the unraveling of "this indefinite knot" of power relations, a strategy that would result in an effective political critique freed from Imaginary identifications.

Such a strategy would have to constitute itself as some-

2. Ibid., p. 168.

thing more than a simple opposition to existing paradigms of critical activity. The entire framework of basic presuppositions has to be discarded in order to bring about the mere possibility of a real change in this realm of intellectual endeavor. The failure to do so explains the inadequacy of all the well-meaning projects of reform based on humanistic solutions since "humanism is based on the desire to change the ideological system without altering institutions; and reformers wish to change the institution without touching the ideological system" (*LCMP,* p. 228). These projects derive from the melioristic and optimistic outlook that marked the Enlightenment. The eighteenth century has handed down the belief in a progress that is made possible by the advancement and dissemination of disinterested knowledge but, as Foucault observes, "there is no point in dreaming of a time when knowledge will cease to depend on power; this is just a way of reviving humanism in a utopian guise" (*PK,* p. 52). From Foucault's standpoint, significant changes are not possible within the framework of the principal models of political action we have inherited from the eighteenth and nineteenth centuries; in this regard, as Alan Sheridan has observed, "Foucault's 'political anatomy' is the clearest and most fully developed version of a new political 'theory' and 'practice' that is just beginning to emerge from the discrediting of both Marxism and 'reformism.' "[3] Foucault's writings partake, then, of a growing awareness that the current versions of reform or revolution are liable only to reproduce all the familiar strategies of exploitation and control.

Furthermore, within the anthropological arrangement of power-knowledge strategies, the more radical and reform claims to be, the more severe the disillusionment brought about by the results. Such is the case of revolutions that take place without effecting any significant changes at the level of power-knowledge configurations. The Russian Revolution

3. Alan Sheridan, *Michel Foucault: The Will to Truth* (London: Tavistock. 1980), pp. 221–22.

has thus replaced one class of exploiters by another—only more violent—and, while changing the rhetoric of the system, has reappropriated the fundamental modalities of bourgeois culture: "In Soviet society one has the example of a State apparatus which has changed hands, yet leaves social hierarchies, family life, sexuality and the body more or less as they were in capitalist society" (*PK*, p. 73). The case of the Russian Revolution poses an especially perplexing problem, since it represents an example of a fascist system that has evolved under the cover of a leftist ideology. From the critical standpoint that Foucault wishes to elaborate, Western capitalism and Soviet socialism do not represent a significant opposition. While the two camps have thrived on regularly denouncing each other, "the mechanisms of power in themselves were never analyzed" (*PK*, p. 116). As a consequence, Foucault finds that "the non-analysis of fascism is one of the important political facts of the past thirty years. It enables fascism to be used as a floating signifier" (*PK*, p. 139). The question then becomes one of reconciling the critiques of both Western capitalism and Socialist totalitarianism and of relating "concretely, both in analysis and in practice, the critique of the technologies of normalization which derive historically from Classical internment with the struggle against the historically growing threat posed by the Soviet Gulag" (*PK*, p. 137).

Quite understandably, Foucault's attitude toward Marxism is ambivalent. On the one hand, he recognizes the value of a Marxist critique, finding that it is impossible to write effectively about history without using the terminology and concepts developed by Marx—a language that has become an integral part of our thinking. On the other hand, Foucault believes all attempts to resuscitate Marx to be futile at best and considers the massive discursive activity that has evolved "around a proper name, signifying at once a certain individual, the totality of his writings, and an immense historical process deriving from him" (*PK*, p. 76) to be of use strictly for academic exercises. As for practical applications, they are possible only in terms of "a game whose rules aren't Marxist but communistological, in other words defined by communist parties who decide how you must use Marx so as to be declared by them to be a Marxist" (*PK*, p. 53). Furthermore, we have already seen that Foucault considers Marxism to be flawed by its anthropocentric and teleological emphases. Marxism produces ontological terms that serve to occlude crucial aspects of social reality; the concept of a dominant class explains very little, for example, since "anything can be deduced from the general phenomenon of the domination of the bourgeois class. What needs to be done is something quite different" (*PK*, p. 100). The strategy that Foucault proposes does not start "from the top" as it were, by positing sovereign principles such as "history" or "class"— concepts that have been explained as soon as they have been produced—but approaches the question of social existence from below, by examining the micro-mechanisms of power, the minute strategies that involve bodies living their everyday life.

This strategic inversion is produced by the conviction that systems of domination are made operative by those discourses that revolve around certain slogans and key words— terms whose unquestioned prestige allows the imposition of cultural and economic hegemonies. Even the seemingly fundamental concepts that have distinguished Western civilization are to be discarded because "these notions of human nature, of justice, of the realization of the essence of human beings, are all notions and concepts which have been formed within our civilization, within our type of knowledge and our form of philosophy, and that as a result form part of our class system."[4] Ultimately, all attempts to provide social systems with a theoretical framework have to be abandoned and theory as such is to be repudiated since "this need for

4. Elders, *Reflexive Water*, p. 187.

theory is still part of the system we reject" (*LCMP*, p. 231). Any attempt to conceive intellectually of a new system will only prepare the terrain for a modified version of the old one, a contrivance that will still operate in terms of an order, of hierarchies and discipline, of processes of selection, exclusion, domination, and exploitation. Theory not only ties us to the basic pattern of power-knowledge strategies that marks the present system, but also creates the misleading dichotomy of theory and practice, a duality implying that the two terms represent clearly separate entities. In fact, theory is a mode of practice, although a surreptitious one, since it hides its practical effects under the mantle of pure intellectualism. This strategy is particularly evident in the case of "science," the form of intellectual activity that enjoys the greatest prestige in our society because it appears most disinterested, most "objective," most likely to produce truth.

To be sure, it is not science as such that Foucault attacks; rather it is the privileged position enjoyed by the sciences, especially those seeking to determine man's place in society —a position that has given them the power of establishing a certain "régime of truth." Foucault is therefore "opposed primarily not to the contents, methods or concepts of a science, but to the effects of the centralizing powers which are linked to the institution and functioning of an organized scientific discourse within a society such as ours" (*PK*, p. 84). Discourses that aim to achieve or that already claim a scientific status implicitly downgrade and disqualify competing discourses of knowledge; they are involved in a political strategy and instead of being accepted as impartial quests for truth, they should be posed these incriminating questions: "Which speaking, discoursing subjects—which subjects of experience and knowledge—do you then want to 'diminish' when you say: 'I who conduct this discourse am conducting a scientific discourse, and I am a scientist'? Which theoretical-political *avant garde* do you want to enthrone in order to isolate it from all the discontinuous forms of knowledge that circulate about it?" (*PK*, p. 85). Whether it is Marxism, or psychoanalysis, or some other systematic construct, as soon as it claims scientific status it is seeking to establish a global and totalizing theoretical domination; its aim is then to set up a new grid for distinguishing truth from falsehood and for producing a strategy of power inseparably linked to the truth it promotes. The question therefore becomes one of outlining the "politics of truth" operative in each systematic attempt to represent the social existence of man—"not a matter of emancipating truth from every system of power (which would be a chimera, for truth is already power) but of detaching the power of truth from the forms of hegemony, social, economic, and cultural, within which it operates at the present time" (*PK*, p. 133). Innovation within the same modality of knowledge-power formation is not possible, attempting to change ideologies or affect consciousnesses is futile; it is the modality itself, with all the attending notions of theory, knowledge, and truth, that has to be dispersed.

At the same time, it may be practical to retain certain elements of the traditional approaches. Certain strategies or concepts borrowed from Marxism or psychoanalysis may well be used as tools of analysis or research, but only on condition that they be disconnected from the theoretical matrix that has supported them, that is, from the dogmatic pretense of teleological and all-embracing explanations; the founding theoretical unity of these systems would thus be "put in abeyance, or at least curtailed, divided, overthrown, caricatured, theatricalized" (*PK*, p. 81). The retained elements would then be applied in a fragmentary, localized, and incidental manner. Such would also be the manner of the critical approach that Foucault envisages. It would be an activity designed in response to specific local conditions, a strategy circumscribed by a consideration of attending historical, economic, and political circumstances. No longer would there be an appeal to the higher authority of an established regime of thought, to the guarantee of a transcendent morality or ideology.

Without the support of a universal design, a totalizing system, or a supreme code, the intellectual can claim to be neither prophet nor guru, neither judge nor priest. He cannot pretend to play the role of the grand statesman-strategist or that of the wise teacher–guide for the unenlightened masses. The model of the eighteenth-century philosophe, with its implicit intellectual and moral superiority, is no longer relevant because the masses know quite well by themselves. Furthermore, in spite of his claims, the intellectual is really incapable of dealing with the complexity of a society taken in its totality; he is hopelessly lost in the face of certain social upheavals—occasions when the inadequacy of his systems is particularly glaring. Such an inadequacy was amply demonstrated in May 1968 when, according to Foucault, the intellectual discovered that "the masses no longer need him to gain knowledge: they *know* perfectly well, without illusion; they know far better than he and they are certainly capable of expressing themselves" (*LCMP*, p. 207). What the people *know* constitutes what Foucault calls "historical" or "fragmentary" knowledges. These knowledges arise in an unsystematic, haphazard manner and are not tied to any official systems of knowledge—precisely the systems maintained by the intellectuals, who have thus accepted the role of agents of established interests.

Foucault thus appears to have uncovered a new version of the inevitable "trahison des clercs." The perspective provided by his analysis leads us to suppose that if intellectuals saw more clearly the effects of their activity, they would face up to their inveterate insufficiency, abandon their pretense of superiority and expertise, and, instead of contributing chimerical systems that only serve to maintain patterns of domination, they would make their work benefit the people, since "power is always exercised at the expense of the people" (*LCMP*, p. 211). An intellectual wishing to serve the cause of

the masses would side with those who resist hegemonic
domination: not, however, as a leader or as a spiritual guide
but by simply "doing the job" for which he is trained:

> The intellectual no longer has to play the role of an advisor.
> The project, tactics and goals to be adopted are a matter for
> those who do the fighting. What the intellectual can do is to
> provide instruments of analysis, and at present this is the his-
> torian's essential role. What's effectively needed is a ramified,
> penetrative perception of the present, one that makes it possi-
> ble to locate lines of weakness, strong points, positions where
> the instances of power have secured and implanted themselves
> by a system of organization dating back over 150 years. In
> other words, a topological and geological survey of the battle-
> field—that is the intellectual's role. But as for saying, "Here is
> what you must do!," certainly not. (PK, p. 62)

Foucault's own archaeological and genealogical approaches
are conceived as useful strategies, not for elaborating explanations or revealing the transcendental project that oversees
our history and our civilization, but for exposing the mechanisms that have been instrumental in setting up the existing
systems of knowledge. Foucault has no intention of design-
ing a program of action or setting up some ideal model to
emulate; he therefore refuses to engage in visionary specu-
lation: "I admit to not being able to define, nor for even
stronger reasons to propose, an ideal social model for the
functioning of our scientific or technological society. On the
other hand, one of the tasks that seems immediate and urgent to me, over and above anything else, is this: that we
should indicate and show up, even where they are hidden,
all the relationships of political power which actually control
the social body and oppress and repress it."[5] There is obviously a need for some theoretical framework for such a
task; however, the function Foucault envisages for theory in
political undertakings of this sort differs radically from the

5. Ibid., pp. 170–71.

major roles theory has usually been given: "The role for theory today seems to me to be just this: not to formulate the global systematic theory which holds everything in place, but to analyze the specificity of mechanisms of power, to locate the connections and extensions, to build little by little a strategic knowledge (*savoir*)" (*PK*, p. 145). In the context of such a strategy, theory becomes in effect practice: it is immediately applicable for purposes to be determined by those who have a need for it. It does not prescribe a mode of action—it is action. Moreover, such an activity can no longer be considered purely theoretical because it dismantles the very basis for theory in the traditional sense by considering meaning to be a secondary and contingent discursive manifestation. This new theoretical approach is not effectuated at the level of the signifier but from a perspective that reveals discourse to be an event in a network of power relations. Foucault points out that "both the nature of events and the fact of power are invariably excluded from knowledge as presently constituted in our culture"; therefore the approach he seeks to develop will first do away with all the meaningful and misleading categories of discourse, since we use such categories as "truth, man, culture, writing, etc.—to dispel the shock of daily occurrences, to dissolve the event" (*LCMP*, pp. 220–21). The task to be undertaken is the analysis of truth-producing mechanisms.

We have been culturally conditioned to accept truth as a product of officially recognized processes of research carried out by appropriately qualified subjects, but, asks Foucault, "what if understanding the relation of the subject to the truth, were just an effect of knowledge? What if understanding were a complex, multiple, non-individual formation, not 'subjected to the subject,' which produced effects of truth? One should then put forward positively this entire dimension which the history of science has negativized."[6] This

6. Ibid., p. 149.

Symbolic dimension of nonindividual formation becomes a positive and uppermost concern for archaeological and genealogical analyses; these approaches seek to emancipate the "local" or "minor" knowledges that do not participate in overall schemes of domination and that can therefore serve to oppose officially established modes of contriving truth-effects: "'Archaeology' would be the appropriate methodology of this analysis of local discursivities, and 'genealogy' would be the tactics whereby, on the basis of the descriptions of these local discursivities, the subjected knowledges which were thus released would be brought into play" (*PK*, p. 85). The effect of such a strategy would be to reveal the rules that are operative in the constitution of knowledges and to disclose the mechanisms of the conventions that bind individuals to particular forms of understanding and that make them apprehend their existence in terms of specific ideological or moral totalities.

Just as Foucault sees the reign of universal theories coming to an end, he considers the role of the "universal" intellectual to be no longer relevant. This role, which has usually been filled in the most exemplary fashion by the "writer of genius," this "bearer of values and significations in which all can recognize themselves," has now given way to that of the "specific" intellectual, the savant or expert. The latter no longer provides guidance or inspiration but exercises a vital function in a field of endeavor that has a strategic importance for the well-being, or simply the "being" of humanity. The intellectual no longer represents universal values; "it is rather he who along with a handful of others, has at his disposal, whether in the service of the State or against it, powers which can either benefit or irrevocably destroy life. He is no longer the rhapsodist of the eternal, but the strategist of life and death" (*PK*, p. 129).

Foucault's own activity obviously tends to pale with the crucial functions he attributes to the specific intellectual. Moreover, Foucault's critical endeavors appear even more unimportant in light of his apparent inclination to devalue his own activity. On the one hand, he tends to minimize the consequences of his own enterprise and on the other, by presenting his critical activity as a tool for revealing the rules operative in the game of knowledge, he can propose it as no more than a game itself. Can this kind of intellectual venture possibly rival the prestige of an occupation whose strategists make decisions affecting life and death? And, more significantly, can it have a bearing on such decisions?

9

The Game of Knowledge

Let us suppose then that we have overcome our culturally conditioned predisposition to find the author, his consciousness, and his life behind his writing, and that we agree to consider the *œuvre* of Michel Foucault as an endeavor that seeks to evade traditional patterns. By impelling our thought toward the invisible yet ever-present determinisms of the Symbolic and by disrupting our habitual tendency to provide discourses with the ontological guarantee of Imaginary subjects, Foucault's approach demands that we consider writing as an activity that "unfolds like a game that inevitably moves beyond its own rules and finally leaves them behind. Thus, the essential basis of this writing is not the exalted emotions related to the act of composition or the insertion of a subject into language. Rather, it is primarily concerned with creating an opening where the writing subject endlessly disappears" (*LCMP*, p. 116). Foucault's theory and practice are at one in this regard and his work is predicated on an evasive tactic that produces identity only to dismantle it, on a will to escape identifiable ethical or epistemological determinisms; hence, explains Foucault, "the cautious, stumbling manner of this text: at every turn, it stands back, measures up what is before it, gropes towards its limits, stumbles against what it does not mean, and digs pits to mark out its own path" (*AK*, p. 17). Foucault's writing is at times so tentative that, in a certain sense, it seems to reject its own validity. If at the beginning of *The Archaeology of Knowledge* we read: "I have tried to define this blank space from which I speak, and which is slowly taking shape in a discourse that I feel to be so precarious and so unsure" (p. 17), toward the end, Foucault refuses to grant the reader any frame of reference—not even the work itself:

> My discourse, far from determining the locus in which it speaks, is avoiding the ground on which it could find support. It is a discourse about discourses: but it is not trying to find in them a hidden law, a concealed origin that it only remains to free; nor is it trying to establish by itself, taking itself as a starting-point, the general theory of which they would be the concrete models. It is trying to deploy a dispersion that can never be reduced to a single system of differences, a scattering that is not related to absolute axes of reference; it is trying to operate a decentering that leaves no privilege to any centre. [P. 205]

In this manner, Foucault's discourse anticipates and frustrates all those conventional strategies of reading and interpretation which immediately seek to find a systematicness in a text and try to relate the latter to established forms of knowledge, to accredited sciences, and to official modes of thought.

Thus, an Imaginary subjective reality may well be rendered irrelevant by Foucault's discursive strategy and it may indeed appear pointless to reconcile his work with some psychological or biographical construct named Foucault because, as Foucault himself has pointed out, "what I have said here is not 'what I think,' but often rather what I wonder whether one couldn't think" (*PK*, p. 145). Such a statement should not be shrugged off as a Foucaldian mannerism, for it is much more than a vague affectation: it provides an apt illustration for the Lacanian aphorism—"I *am* there where *I* do not *think*." It also reemphasizes the commitment that Foucault's discourse maintains with regard to the Symbolic and points to the Symbolic mediation that is operative in the act of writing—a mediation of which the authorial self has to be constantly aware. We are left then with the *function* of subject, a specific role that is attributable to the author and one that the discourse defines for itself as the necessary and constitutive element of its own reality. In the case of Michel Foucault, such a function may well appear problematic, since his discourse advocates a ludic strategy, yet frequently adopts a stance that seems to imply that it is making certain moral and political claims. It is inevitable that we question the status and the potential effect of such a discourse and that we seek to determine whether this discourse is really useful or whether it is simply gratuitous, whether the intellectual role it sustains represents an earnest or a cynical critical approach to the issues it raises.

Reduced to its general and superficial appearances, Foucault's discourse could be described as an attempt to discredit traditional approaches to culture, as an attack on the two principal modalities of Western discursive practice: the humanistic and the scientific. These two are found to be the principal modes of domination and subjection in Western societies: humanism constructs sovereign subjects, themes of human essence that permit the subsequent elaboration of scientific strategies of investigation, control, and normalization. It is in this context that discourses establish networks of power-knowledge relations that benefit certain segments of a society. The bourgeoisie has thus been able to establish its particular "régime of truth," a discursive practice that functions both to maintain its class advantages and to provide an ethical justification for its economic privileges. For Foucault therefore, "the problem is not changing people's consciousnesses—or what's in their heads—but the political, economic, institutional régime of the production of truth" (*PK*, p. 133). Hence the necessity for avoiding all the traditional epistemological approaches, which only serve to reintegrate criticism within the existing cultural hegemony. However, although Foucault's discourse does appear to have

effectively undermined the strategies that have been fundamental in maintaining a certain power-knowledge configuration in Western culture, the significant factor may well seem
to be his own intellectual position in the framework of this
culture: in spite of its antagonistic stance, his discourse could
very well be considered yet another brilliant example of a
critical tradition that functions merely to illustrate and up-
hold the superiority of a bourgeois civilization. Obviously,
Foucault's own position and status could be characterized as
those of a bourgeois intellectual. His discourse, an academic
exercise produced for the benefit of other bourgeois, of other
university professors, could be viewed as carrying out an
essential function in the ecology of a bourgeois cultural system, by formulating a critique that is sufficiently convincing
in its condemnation of social inequities to ensure the moral
tranquillity—and validity—of the whole system.

Of course, Foucault claims to support the cause of the
proletariat—of those who are without status, without privileges, and without recognition, of those who are disenfran-
chised, alienated, or excluded. In addition, he finds that a
rapprochement between intellectuals and those at the bottom
of the social scale is not based on idle sentiment but has
actually taken place: "I believe intellectuals have actually
been drawn closer to the proletariat and the masses, for two
reasons. Firstly, because it has been a question of real, material, everyday struggles, and secondly because they have
often been confronted, albeit in a different form, by the same
adversary as the proletariat, namely the multinational cor-
porations, the judicial and police apparatuses, the property
speculators, etc." (PK, p. 126). Yet it could be argued that
the mode in which the common people perceive this "adversary" is probably quite different from the way in which
the intellectual experiences the confrontation. The latter is
after all protected by a certain economic and social status
which allows him to enjoy a life of reflection and which
shelters him from the immediate brutality of a common ex-

istence, an everyday reality the lower classes have to face in a manner that is neither theoretical nor philosophical. What sustains the common people is often the hope of achieving a bourgeois level of comfort and freedom and the concerns of a Foucault might well appear highly irrelevant in such a context. Foucault, we know, is concerned, obsessed even, with the question of power:

> What is at stake in all these genealogies is the nature of this power which has surged into view in all its violence, aggression and absurdity in the course of the last forty years, contemporaneously, that is, with the collapse of Fascism and the decline of Stalinism. What, we must ask, is this power—or rather, since that is to give a formulation to the question that invites the kind of theoretical coronation of the whole which I am so keen to avoid—what are these various contrivances of power, whose operations extend to such differing levels and sectors of society and are possessed of such manifold ramifications? What are their mechanisms, their effects and their relations? [*PK*, pp. 87–88]

It is likely that for those who feel powerless in society there is nothing absurd nor mysterious about power: its mechanisms, effects, and relations are only too clear and what really counts is achieving a more privileged status, such as that enjoyed by the likes of Foucault—a position that allows one to adopt a scholastic view of power.

We are thus faced with the general question of the effectiveness and usefulness of a discourse such as that of Foucault, with the problem of reconciling its critical intent with its protected status. One possible approach would be to view it in terms of a situation similar to that of certain forms of illegality: since it does not really threaten anything essential in the system, its existence is made possible by "a simple relaxation on the part of the system which, aware of its own solidity, can afford to accept at its margins something which after all poses absolutely no threat to it" (*PK*, p. 43). According to such a perspective, the marginality of Foucault's discourse would be what makes it acceptable in the context of a bourgeois system, but it also would make it completely ineffective as a contribution to the cause of all those who lead marginal existences. This circumstance could also explain the great prestige, even popularity of Foucault's discourse: it succeeds in combining two basic conditions of achieving intellectual eminence in a bourgeois culture—it effectively conceals its innocuous nature under the apparent radicalness of its critique.

Such an argument would be plausible, were it not for one essential piece of evidence: the fundamentally Symbolic thrust of Foucault's writing. Foucault, we have seen, intends to disrupt the power mechanisms that obtain in Western societies by disclosing the contingency of the truths that validate discourses, by introducing "the point of view of understanding, of its rules, of its systems, of its transformations of totalities in the game of individual knowledge."[1] His approach does not posit substantial, therefore Imaginary, class divisions, identifiable groups with specific consciousnesses; instead, it finds social stratifications already present in individual knowledge-formations. His critique is therefore not aimed at a specific and readily identifiable group, and it does not seek to rescue or to uplift the downtrodden: it is aimed at the circumstances that favor the formation of classes, that make possible domination and exploitation—those circumstances that in some way block the mediating effect of the Symbolic order, that disguise or ignore the mediation of the Symbolic between the self and manifestations of the self, between man and world, between men.

Foucault is obviously not the first nor the only writer to point to an awareness as old as civilization; it is nevertheless an awareness that seems to be increasingly elided in the modern world—a world in which it is often convenient, but dangerous, to forget that our existence depends upon circumstances and is maintained by discourses we do not control but control us, to ignore that "rationality is a means of

1. Fons Elders, *Reflexive Water* (London: Souvenir Press, 1974), p. 151.

domination, an instrument of submission and tyranny, that the cult of meaning leads to the sacrifice of the person in favor of the individual, of the tenor to the vehicle, of the essence to the function, of man and woman to Mankind."[2] It is this ignorance of the Symbolic that makes men prisoners of the images they have formed of themselves or that are imposed upon them; the occultation of the Symbolic establishes truths by producing the illusion of an unmediated contact between consciousness and the Real.

Just as Foucault's discourse does not do away with "man" but only relocates the human outside the constraints of an anthropology, it does not so much discard the subject as it redefines the subjective function of man in the context of discourse. Indeed, man is the subject of Foucault's discourse, a subject that serves, as Lacan puts it, both as a relay for the Symbolic and as a support for it. Man forms an identity in the Imaginary but also requires the Symbolic to transcend this identity, which is felt to be an inadequate representation of the Real; and if he is not bound to his image by an essence or a nature that subjects him to a sovereign cultural order, he is free to reinvest the self in a dependency on the Symbolic: thus, "there is always a reciprocity in [this] dependency and it seems correct to say that man transcends 'himself' as much as he is transcended by the inveiglement of the Symbolic."[3] Man no longer can find his truth in God, nor can he discover it in man; no longer determined by either a divine or an anthropological transcendentalism, he finds himself bound to the fate of all mankind, to the determinisms of the Symbolic order—of what mediates between him and others, between him and his universe.

If an ethical impulse were to be uncovered behind Foucault's writing, it could perhaps be termed a morality of the Symbolic, which could in turn be defined as a will to empha-

2. Renaud Zuppinger, "*Post Coitem Tristitiae:* About a Would-Be Aftermath of Structuralism," *New Literary History* 13, no. 3 (Spring 1982), p. 482.
3. Anika Lemaire, *Jacques Lacan* (Brussels: Pierre Mardaga, 1977), p. 278.

size the meaninglessness of all human activity—but also as a desire to make manifest the unlimited human potential for creating meaning. Accordingly, Foucault elaborates his own discourse in a manner that highlights its own aleatory nature, and even though he cannot avoid a certain systematicness and organization, this order is to be viewed as a fabrication, nothing more. Thus the parallelism between sexuality and criminality that can be brought out in his last two works is simply "the stake in the game"; furthermore, explains Foucault, "if I'm thinking of writing six volumes, it's precisely because it's a game!" (*PK*, p. 209). It is in its rejection of any form of closure that Foucault's approach poses a threat to any system that maintains itself because its truths are taken seriously as authentic representations of the Real. Foucault's strategy presents a marked contrast with the position intellectuals have traditionally assumed: a Foucaldian position refuses to provide an all-embracing perspective in which order and coherence become manifest, but recognizes only fragments, various segments that are localized according to the specific rules that have determined them and according to the economy of discourses in which they fit. This position is further enhanced by Foucault's awareness of the ambiguity to which he is subject as an author and critic: situated between his archive and his audience, he serves as both a conduit for the Symbolic force of discourses around him and a promoter of the power his own discursive practice generates. In this regard, the intellectual stance Foucault illustrates can be construed as an eminently reasonable approach to the game of knowledge: as Edward Said notes, "Learning and, consequently, writing, as the author alternates between them, exemplify the cycle of repetition and beginning, but it is when the distance between them is not made either into a fetish or a commodity (called, with market-oriented affirmation, originality or creativity) that they lead to knowledge and freedom."[4]

4. Edward W. Said, "An Ethics of Language," *Diacritics* 4, no. 2 (Summer 1974), 37.

Archaeology and genealogy do not, however, lend themselves to a facile methodology, as the ludic motif might suggest—on the contrary. It is the traditional approach that has the luxury of occluding significant aspects of its inquiry, when it posits ontological categories that protect it from having to go outside its own Imaginary limits and from questioning the very foundations of its own project. Since it is the process of conceptualization that Foucault wishes to investigate, concepts in and of themselves do not provide answers or explanations. Thus, for example, he finds that the notion of class is insufficient for explaining domination "because this domination is not simply the expression in political terms of economic exploitation, it is its instrument and, to a large extent, the condition which makes it possible; the suppression of the one is achieved through the exhaustive discernment of the other."[5] In order to accomplish such an "exhaustive discernment," Foucault pursues an approach and a strategy that require not only what he has termed a "relentless erudition" (*LCMP*, p. 140), because they intend to disclose the connections linking the topic under investigation to its *episteme* and its archive, but also a constant awareness of the links this investigation effects with its own archive. In this regard, Foucault's discourse manifests the kind of consistency that Lacan finds only in those "discourses in which truth is lame and precisely because they display its lameness, by contrast, there is the inanity of the discourse of knowledge, when affirming itself in its closure it makes liars out of the others. This indeed is the procedure of academic discourse when it makes a thesis of this fiction it calls an author, or of the history of thought, or of something that distinguishes itself in the name of some progress."[6]

Such consistency, however, may well be devoid of any real potential for developing an effective and practical critical strategy. There is no underlying rationale, no specific pro-

---

5. Elders, *Reflexive Water*, p. 172.
6. Preface, by Lacan, to Lemaire, *Jacques Lacan*, pp. 6–7.

gram to motivate this criticism—only a will to undermine, to discredit power in all its manifestations and to dismantle various modes of subjection. Can such an undertaking be anything more than a largely futile intellectual game? In the face of the overpowering amount of cultural indoctrination, social conditioning, economic and political controls, what could possibly be achieved by an approach that is riddled with self-doubt and lacks the fundamental coherence and conviction of the Imaginary systems it opposes? Under the conditions that prevail in a university, in a technocratic society, a Foucaldian critical enterprise appears doomed from the start because, as Foucault himself realizes, "after all, is it not perhaps the case that these fragments of genealogies are no sooner brought to light, that the particular elements of the knowledge that one seeks to disinter are no sooner accredited and put into circulation, than they run the risk of re-codification, re-colonization?" (*PK*, p. 86). The most radical strategies of subversion are voided as soon as they become fashionable attitudes or when they are made into academic subjects "as something that distinguishes itself in the name of some progress." Besides, are the problems there where Foucault thinks they are, or is it perhaps possible to speak so abundantly of power, of sexuality, and of the other subjects he treats only because they are nowhere to be found, because these notions no longer pertain to a present social reality? Could Foucault himself be in some ways contributing to the problems he believes he is confronting? These are, as well, some of the questions raised by the critics of Foucault's enterprise. A rapid survey of certain critical postures will help us gauge more effectively the impact and the potential of his achievement.

10

Critical Reactions
and Challenges

Taken as an intellectual event, the work of Michel Foucault is both an integral and an antagonistic part of its cultural archive. It is a brilliant illustration of a French critical tradition and, at the same time, a subversion of some fundamental premises inherent in this tradition. On the one hand, Foucault's stance can be seen to embody a Nietzschean rejection of sense and to represent a trend that Vincent Descombes has characterized as, precisely, "the *nihilism* of Foucault's generation." The term "nihilism," however, is not really even a convenient label since the intellectual strategy exemplified by archaeology and genealogy is in many respects an affirmative and committed approach to human affairs. It is an approach that recognizes culture principally in terms of the exclusions, rejections, and limitations that constitute the foundations of its identity. Thus, Foucault's *œuvre* is equally representative of a general campaign that the philosophers of the so-called structuralist era have waged against the "logic of identity," understood as "that form of thought which cannot represent the *other* to itself without reducing it to the *same,* and thereby subordinating difference to identity."[1] The perspective offered by the dichotomy of the Same

1. Vincent Descombes, *Modern French Philosophy* (Cambridge: Cambridge University Press, 1980), p. 75. The French title of Descombes's work is, significantly, *Le même et l'autre.* For a thorough discussion of this important

and the Other is also, I would like to propose, very useful when it comes to gauging Foucault's contribution to contemporary critical thought. It is a dichotomy reflected not only in the work of Foucault itself, but in the critical debate springing up in the wake of its publication.

It was the publication of *The Order of Things* that brought renown to Foucault; that book has also given rise to more controversy than any of his other writings. Generally speaking, the debate revolved around the fundamental question of identity versus difference, for this seemed to be the crucial issue: did Foucault's perspective represent anything really new, anything really useful, or did archaeology simply refurbish some already familiar approaches? Of course, not everyone felt that it was possible to reach very clear conclusions in this regard and Michel de Certeau noted that most critics of the work "proceed with caution in this still uncertain territory, even if it is to cover it with praise."[2] But some arrived at a quick verdict; Sartre found nothing new or especially surprising in the book and shrugged it off as only "the latest barrier that the bourgeoisie has been able to erect against Marx."[3] For Sartre, Foucault's work was ideological in nature since it wished to deny history: failing to surpass or outdo Marx, Foucault had simply suppressed the truth of Marxism. Henri Lefebvre was equally scornful and wondered whether Foucault's "system" would remain standing very long—especially after it had eliminated the traditional supports of discourse: "Who is speaking in this philosophical discourse, in this *System*? We don't know anymore. It isn't God (he is dead), nor man (a fiction, a representation), nor the individual (another fiction, an illusion of subjectivity), nor, of course, 'I,' nor Foucault. Who is speaking? It's they

book, see Philip Lewis, "The Post-structuralist Condition," *Diacritics* 12, no. 1 (Spring 1982).

2. Michel de Certeau, "Les sciences humaines et la mort de l'homme," *Etudes* 326 (March 1967), 357–358.

3. "Jean-Paul Sartre répond," *L'Arc* 30 (1966), 88.

[on]. There is language. The System. Since there is signification and meaning only inside the System, the System has
no meaning. . . . Through all these discourses and these
'rigorous writings,' the System converses with itself about
itself."[4] The comments offered by Sartre and Lefebvre were
thus part of a general tendency to "demystify the demysti-
fyers," and belonged to a critical strategy purporting to reveal the empty pretense of Foucault's enterprise, arguing
that his book is but "a poem of the antipoetic, a myth of the
antimythical."[5]

Of course, such reactions also reveal the highly disturb-
ing impact of Foucault's writings. If Foucault's book had
indeed touched a critical nerve, it did so because it had
problematized the realm of the intellect by questioning the
very possibility of understanding our historical and philosophical reality. Archaeology had scandalized some because
it was aimed at the sacred institutions of History and Philosophy and because it was attempting to demystify the relation
between the two by establishing, as Georges Canguilhem
put it, "the condition of another history, in which the concept of event is preserved, but in which events affect concepts and not men."[6] Foucault's approach was therefore wel-
comed by some as an adequate expression of a realization
characterizing modern man—a being who knows, in Yves
Bertherat's words, that "his truth may very well be situated
outside of him, and that his self, with all its resistances and
illusions, denies this truth."[7] The distinction between a *cogito*
and an "unthought" had led to the recognition of a "pensée
du dehors," to a thought of the Other; and the ascendancy of
the unconscious over the conscious, of system over the event,

4. Henri Lefebvre, *Position: Contre les technocrates* (Paris: Editions Gonthier,
1967), p. 87.
5. Jean-Marie Domenach, "Le système et la personne," *Esprit*, no. 360
(May 1967), p. 779; Lefebvre, p. 99.
6. Georges Canguilhem, "Mort de l'homme ou épuisement du cogito?"
Critique, no. 242 (July 1967), p. 600.
7. Yves Bertherat, "La pensée folle," *Esprit*, no. 360 (May 1967), p. 863.

of the unthought over thought had thus been revealed by a revolt against reason, by the forceful, terroristic intervention of Foucault: "The action of driving *homo rationalis* out of his regular territory, of analyzing him as an ethnological object, of making classical reason into a 'pensée sauvage,' of killing the *homo* of humanism," wrote Michel Serres, "amounts to a decolonization by means of a terroristic concept of culture, that is to say a reverse colonization."[8]

Judging from the pronouncements of both detractors and admirers, it was evident that Foucault's thought had achieved a telling effect. For some, this effect appeared unduly threatening, and although there were critics who considered Foucault's enterprise a salutary campaign against the "terrorism of reason," others became wary of a philosophical terrorism they perceived in a rapidly spreading antirationalism. These were philosophers who manifested an evident skepticism with regard to what Jean-Marie Domenach called "certain abusive forms of criticism" which intended to break "this essential link between life and thought."[9] They detected a certain intellectual intolerance in Foucault's thought and attributed it to an impatience with an aporia that characterizes the human condition: "The thought of man," wrote Mikel Dufrenne, "always faces the exhausting task of going back from the thought to the thinker; everything it says about man, is said by man, and this man is man only through that which isn't he, through the life of him and the culture around him, . . . he is always other, the other of others, and the other of his self: subject when he is object, object when he is subject."[10] To overcome this inevitable paradox, Foucault had simply elided the notion of man—an action that gave rise to two objections: first, such a move could prefigure an unbearable dogmatism; second, it gave an unlimited pre-

8. Michel Serres, *Hermès I. La communication* (Paris: Minuit, 1968), p. 197.
9. Domenach, p. 780.
10.. Mikel Dufrenne, "La philosophie du néo-positivisme," *Esprit*, no. 360 (May 1967), p. 783.

ponderance to an all-pervasive and all-powerful system which allegedly dominates man and everything he says or does, which speaks and is perceivable through him. But, as Dufrenne pointed out, it was possible to see things differently and to suppose that "man thinks himself only as much as he wishes himself; this does not necessarily mean that anthropology is inspired by ethics or is subordinated to them; theory and practice can be evenly matched and indiscernible provided the value of being is recognized, or rather, provided being is recognized as the fundamental value."[11] Thus, by reestablishing the value of being, man would once more gain an autonomy of intention and of consciousness while the notion of a system would find itself demystified.

Nevertheless, the majority of the critics concerned with the implications of the "death of man" considered this question irremediably linked to the existence of a system, that is, to language. It seemed undeniable to some that the truth inherent in a particular cultural organization, as Certeau put it, "escapes those who collaborate to this culture. Relations predetermine subjects and make them signify something different from what they think they're saying or maintaining." It was therefore important to understand that it was not so much man whose end Foucault proclaimed, as "the end of a certain concept of man who thought he had resolved by means of the positivism of 'human sciences' (this 'refusal of a negative thought') the ever-present problem of death."[12] The theme of the death of man was seen in a positive sense as a search for a new kind of humanism, a new hope, and, wrote Canguilhem, "if the face of man were to be erased from knowledge . . . , there is nothing in Foucault that would let us suppose that he considers this possibility as the sign of a regression."[13] Foucault's intention was interpreted as a will to valorize a man both conscious of his finitude and wishing

11. Ibid., p. 782.
12. Certeau, pp. 357–358.
13. Canguilhem, p. 604.

to transcend the limitations inherent in his knowledge, a man who discovered himself, in Pierre Burgelin's description, as "the author of all knowledge, the builder of all science, a subject facing objects, but himself an object of his own knowledge, in this equivocal situation in which, according to Foucault's own words, he finally exists assuming his own transcendence inside a finitude that he no longer derives from infinity."[14]

Although Foucault's work was seen to mark the end of an era, it was not at all clear what tangible changes the new epistemological configuration would bring since, Bertherat noted, "concerning that which is to come—probably the return of the gods, that is the patient reconstruction of a common myth, of hope—the author of *The Order of Things* can tell us nothing from the vantage where he finds himself."[15] There was, of course, the possibility, Certeau pointed out, that Foucault was himself developing a mythical discourse because "to speak of the death that founds all language still does not take into account and perhaps even avoids the death that threatens this discourse itself."[16] But in general, the critics favorable to Foucault's enterprise offered no conclusions, no definitive interpretations, realizing, as Canguilhem phrased it, that they were dealing with "an explorer and not with a missionary of modern culture."[17] Refusing to look for a new dogma, these writers appreciated the heuristic value of Foucault's archaeological model and looked forward to further elaborations and eventual sequels to *The Order of Things.*

If the publication of *The Order of Things* had been marked by an intense, almost frantic critical activity, the appearance of *The Archaeology of Knowledge* provoked a relatively small amount of reaction. It was found to be a disconcerting work:

14. Pierre Burgelin, "L'archéologie du savoir," *Esprit*, no. 360 (May 1967), p. 860.
15. Bertherat, p. 879.
16. Certeau, p. 360.
17. Canguilhem, p. 604.

first of all because it was nearly impossible to discuss it by applying traditional criteria and methods of critical inquiry. Some were therefore content to shrug it off and hope that this "new fashion will blow away like smoke" just as other fashionable trends, such as existentialism, had blown away after a period of intellectual overbearance.[18] Another approach consisted again in comparing archaeology to established— and preferable—systems of thought, such as Marxism. Dominique Lecourt thus found that "the most positive aspect of *The Archaeology of Knowledge* is its attempt to inaugurate, under the rubric of 'discursive formation,' a materialistic and historical theory pertaining to ideological relations and the formation of ideological objects." Foucault had failed, however, to resolve the problem of distinguishing between discursive and nondiscursive practices and to analyze adequately the mechanisms linking the two. His project in this regard was only a beginning, and his theories needed to be "reworked on the solid ground of historical materialism."[19]

One essay stood out in its opposition to all such attempts at downgrading archaeology's claims: the article by Gilles Deleuze in *Critique*. Contrary to such critics as Lecourt, Deleuze felt that, with the delineation of *énoncés* and the archive, "something new, profoundly new, has been born in philosophy." Deleuze's essay was a remarkable analysis of *The Archaeology of Knowledge* because it did not resort to any familiar mechanisms of interpretation. Thus, it found that what was essential in Foucault's work was the discovery and the exploration of "this *unknown land* where a literary form, a scientific proposition, an everyday sentence, a schizophrenic nonsense, etc., are *equally énoncés*, without having anything in common, without undergoing a discursive reduction or

18. Louis Millet and Madeleine Varin d'Ainvelle, *Le structuralisme* (Paris: Editions Universitaires, 1970), pp. 78–79.

19. Dominique Lecourt, *Pour une critique de l'épistémologie* (Paris: François Maspéro, 1972), pp. 113, 124, 130. See also Sheridan's discussion of Lecourt's critique in *Michel Foucault: The Will to Truth* (London: Tavistock, 1980), pp. 214–217.

equivalency. It is this point that had never been reached, by logicians, formalists, or interpreters." Deleuze also supposed that the success of this "theoretical" enterprise resulted from the fact that it was really not one at all and that Foucault had indeed managed to avoid a procedure that could have been considered traditional, that is, a theorization, a rationalization of the method applied in his earlier works. In this sense, Foucault's archaeology possessed a poetic dimension. Paradoxically, such poetry could have practical consequences as well since it was not only radical from an intellectual point of view but was also politically innovative: it represented "a call for a general theory of productions, a theory which must fuse with a revolutionary practice, in which the acting discourse is formed in the element of an 'outside' that is indifferent to my life and to my death."[20] It is thus already possible to discern, adumbrated in Deleuze's critique, the theme of discursive practices implicated in strategies of power and dependent on a Symbolic "outside" that oversees the organization of power-knowledge strategies.

Deleuze was equally receptive to *Discipline and Punish*, finding that "it's as if, finally, something new had emerged since Marx" and that, contrary to Marxism, Foucault's approach offered a real possibility of opposing and disarming mechanisms of power, in particular the "terrifying power of normalization operative in modern societies."[21] Writing in the same issue of *Critique* as Deleuze, François Ewald brought out the liberating effect of Foucault's discourse, which he credited with the potential to reveal the "illusions of truth" that constitute the "political anatomy" of societies and found that Foucault's method was "perhaps the only way of writing a discourse which, for once, would not seek to acquire power but to destroy it." An archaeological strategy succeeded in

20. Gilles Deleuze, "Un nouvel archiviste," *Critique*, no. 274 (March 1970), pp. 195, 202, 206, 208.
21. Gilles Deleuze, "Ecrivain non: Un nouveau cartographe," *Critique*, no. 343 (Dec. 1975), pp. 1211–12.

freeing man in the only way that was truly effective, that is "from man himself and from his humanity."[22] With the publication of *Discipline and Punish* Foucault had become the great authority on the question of power and "to understand what Foucault has contributed to this domain," observed one critic, "I see only one possible comparison, that with Freud. Just as Freud discovered and explored one continent, that of sexuality, Foucault identifies and covers another continent, that of power."[23] Such a paean to Foucault's writings obviously suggests that his thought was beginning not only to gain widespread acceptance but also to exert its own influence as an essential part of the French intellectual establishment. Inevitably, this ascendancy was to invite an attempt to dethrone, to subvert archaeology.

The most ambitious attempt to date is to be found in Jean Baudrillard's *Oublier Foucault*, a fairly abstruse poetico-philosophic essay that indicts Foucault for collusion with prevailing myth-making strategies.[24] Foucault is shown to have become infatuated with the Imaginary force of his own discourse, and his genealogy is depicted as a system satisfying a certain hegemonic logic of reason. The publication of *Oublier Foucault* thus represents a significant confrontation on the French intellectual scene. The book issues a violent challenge to the principal tenets of Foucault's epistemology and attempts to turn on its head its implicit claim of radicalism.

To be sure, the proposal that Foucault be forgotten at a time when he is becoming a cultural monolith also has a humorous ring to it; in addition, while appealing to the icon-

22. François Ewald, "Anatomie et corps politiques," *Critique*, no. 343 (Dec. 1975), pp. 1233, 1260, 1265.

23. Jacques Donzelot, "Misère de la culture politique," *Critique*, nos. 373–374 (June–July 1978), p. 575.

24. The English translation of *Oublier Foucault* (by Nicole Dufresne) has appeared in a special issue, "On Foucault," of *Humanities in Society* 3, no. 1 (Winter 1980).

oclastic strain in each of us, it intimates that we are not to forget Baudrillard. One could, of course argue that Baudrillard's work deserves to be better known, especially in view of the possibly overinflated, fashionable popularity of Foucault's books. It has even been suggested that Baudrillard may be one of the very few contemporary thinkers, perhaps the only one, "able to stand up to Foucault, to discuss his work and to do a real critique of it as equal to equal."[25] The case for Baudrillard is all the more impressive if we consider the entire corpus of his work, the books published both before and after *Oublier Foucault*.[26] What makes this work particularly interesting from our perspective is the suggestion, implicit in *Oublier Foucault*, that Baudrillard's critique of Western civilization is the valid alternative to Foucault's archaeological approach. Since Baudrillard has proposed his *oeuvre* as the Other of Foucault's discourse, it becomes necessary to examine the thrust of his principal arguments. They will serve to define Foucault's position more precisely.

Western civilization has entered the age of hyperreality, a state of existence characterized by the domination of codes. We live in an era of simulation, of simulacra that refer to one another in an unending play of duplication and reflection. The only way out, the only hope, is to push these systems to their limit, to the point where they appear in their hollow absurdity and collapse. This, briefly, is the apocalyptic vision that Baudrillard evokes in *L'échange symbolique et la mort*, his longest and one of his most important works to date. Pub-

25. Antoine Griset, in *Les dieux dans la cuisine* (Paris: Aubier, 1978), p. 54.
26. Baudrillard has published the following works: *Le système des objets* (Paris: Gallimard, 1968); *La société de consommation* (Paris: Denoël, 1970); *Pour une critique de l'économie politique du signe* (Paris: Gallimard, 1972); *Le miroir de la production* (Paris: Casterman, 1973); *L'échange symbolique et la mort* (Paris: Gallimard, 1976); *Oublier Foucault* (Paris: Galilée, 1977); *L'effet Beaubourg: Implosion et dissuasion* (Paris: Galilée, 1977); *A l'ombre des majorités silencieuses ou la fin du social* (Paris: Utopie, 1978); *Le P.C. ou les paradis artificiels* (Paris: Utopie, 1978); *De la séduction* (Paris: Galilée, 1979); *Simulacres et simulation* (Paris: Galilée, 1981).

lished just before *Oublier Foucault*, it can serve to elucidate that work as well as to sum up Baudrillard's general purpose, which has been to unveil the pretenses, the deceits, and the tautologies of the value systems that constitute Western civilization.

Baudrillard's critique is self-consciously radical and takes the form of a theoretical terrorism, engaging in a violent rhetorical campaign aimed at the foundations of Western civilization. At the same time, it voids all other radicalisms, past and present, considering them revolutionary only in the cyclical sense of the term. The epistemological history of our culture is, for Baudrillard, a spiral-shaped evolution of three distinguishable stages, each new loop simply being a reflection, a repetition on a higher level of the system below. Accordingly, the second level is the locus of theoretical critiques of the social realm and is made up of the objectifications and dialectical explanations that interpret linguistic, economic, conscious, and unconscious subjects. The third, at which we have arrived, uses the second-level systems as its referents and is thoroughly dominated by codes that have become its principles of reality. We have been ushered into the era of simulation, of undecidable, commutable values, where distinctions of "the beautiful and the ugly in fashions, of left and right in politics, of truth and falsehood in all the messages of the media, of the useful and the useless at the level of objects, of nature and culture at all levels of signification" are all erased as are "all the great humanistic criteria of value" (*Echange*, p. 21). God, Man, Progress, History, have all died for the benefit of the code, transcendence has given way to immanence, and it is now "the discontinuous indeterminism of the genetic code that governs life— the teleonomical principle" (*Echange*, p. 92). The term teleonomical, which mimics teleological, thus serves to suggest that the familiar scholasticism proposing a divinely ordered universe has been replaced by a faith in the supreme determinative power of words. In addition, dialectical teleologies have given way to molecular play, ideological models have been replaced by the aleatory strategies of both electronic and microbiological cells.[27]

The new strategies have, at the same time, made possible new techniques of control, newer and more efficient modes of socialization. But the new systems do not admit they exist for purposes of social management since "any system, in order to become an end in itself, must put aside the question of its true ends" (*Pour une critique*, p. 71). The new order therefore relies on referents of the second level: "There have always been churches to hide the death of God, or to hide that God was everywhere—which is the same thing. There will always be animal and Indian reservations to conceal that they are dead, and that we are all Indians. There will always be factories to conceal that work is dead, that production is dead, or that it is everywhere and nowhere" (*Echange*, p. 36). Economic and political systems are falling into a binary pattern, thus making possible an illusion of bipolar oppositions and ensuring a stability and durability that monopolies, single political parties, or lone superpowers would not possess standing by themselves. The dual form of our logic is characteristic of the fundamental code that regulates our society; it allows for distinction, opposition, and exclusion, thus determining the processes of simulation that dominate our culture. Such binary articulations, together with a strategy of dissimulation, characterize the development of all contemporary social systems, beginning with the signifying process itself. These systems, in turn, have been instrumental in the creation of a new reality, the reality of codes that are the products of a political economy.

27. Baudrillard ranks Foucault with the advocates of today's scientism, with all the intellectuals who have fallen prey to the world of molecules and the spirals of DNA and who are eager to "rediscover as a mechanism of desire what cyberneticists have described as a codifying and controlling matrix" (*Oublier*, p. 47). The image of Foucault as an accomplice in a grand design of cybernetic control is doubtless outrageous, but outrageous parody, we must remember, is well within Baudrillard's admitted strategy.

The proliferation of codes in modern society has led to a "fetishism of the signifier," an obsession with signifying systems that are fascinating because they provide an "abstract coherence that stitches all contradictions and divisions" (*Pour une critique*, p. 113). At the same time, as we noted above, the signifier requires the justification of a signified, a "natural" foundation that provides a rational, moral, or ideological alibi. Carrying this analysis to the economic level and viewing society in Marxist terms, Baudrillard demonstrates that it is exchange value which is the determining motivation, use value being no more than a post-facto rationalization. In Western societies, the first to be instituted are value systems, which then call forth the necessary concrete referents; the latter are subsequently presented as the motivations and the needs that found our societies. In such a system of political economy, "there is not only a quantitative exploitation of man as productive force by the system of capitalistic political economy, but a metaphysical overdetermination of man as producer by the *code* of the political economy" (*Miroir*, p. 21). As for Marxism, it has only succeeded in perpetuating the myth on which capitalism is founded; as it resorts to a similar metaphor of production, it appeals to "the same fiction, the same naturalization, which is to say, to a convention just as arbitrary, a model of simulation destined to encode all human material, all possibility of desire and exchange in terms of value, of finality, and of production" (*Miroir*, p. 9). Marxism fails to provide an alternative to capitalism because Marx failed to see the collusion linking the order of production to that of representation in Western societies. A radical critique of the latter is possible only if it recognizes that exchange value and the signifier are "the ultimate 'Reason,' the structural principle of the whole system," and that "it is the rational abstraction of the exchange value system and the play of signifiers that rule the whole" (*Pour une critique*, p. 190). As a consequence, it is the capacity to control codes and to manipulate signs that grants political and economic power in our society. This circumstance, in turn, permits the continuous process of accumulation and exploitation that takes place under the aegis of a metaphysics of reason: "The whole repressive and reductive strategy of systems of power is already in the internal logic of the sign, as it is in the internal logic of exchange value and political economy" (*Pour une critique*, p. 199). Therefore, to put an end to the terrorism of rationality that permeates our culture, "the only strategy is a *catastrophical* one, and not at all dialectical. Things must be pushed to their limit, where quite naturally they reverse themselves and collapse" (*Echange*, p. 11). The poetic mode must be enhanced at the expense of rationality, ambiguity must replace the tyranny of sense, of things that "make sense," reversibility must take the place of linearity and accumulation; to these ends, the order of the Symbolic must be granted its preeminence so as to terminate the hegemony of the sign and of value.

For Baudrillard, the Imaginary collusion between signifier and signified, between exchange value and use value, constitutes the order that has become the ruling mode in our culture; consequently, our social consciousness derives its existence from the image reflected by an all-powerful, ever-present discourse of production: "Production, work, value, all that through which an objective world emerges and through which man recognizes himself objectively—all that is the Imaginary in which man is drawn [*embarqué*] in an endless deciphering of himself through his works, finalized by his shadow (his own end), reflected by this operational mirror, this ideal of the productive self, as it were, . . . by the mirror of the political economy" (*Miroir*, p. 9). Man is no longer able to think of himself in terms other than those of production and value, his discourses of production and representation constituting a mirror in the Imaginary—a mirror in which political economy reproduces itself as the determining motivation. Hence the need to break this mirror.

Baudrillard's strategy is thus to deploy theoretical violence, a conscious and purposeful violence aimed in particular at those discourses that are characterized by an ambivalent existence—the discourses that derive from a Symbolic insight but have become entrapped in their own discursive practice. Consequently, the Symbolic meaning of exchange or "the principle of reversion (counter-gift) must be pitted against all the economic, psychological, or structuralist interpretations made possible by Mauss. The Saussure of the *Anagrammes* must be pitted against the Saussure of linguistics, and even against his own narrow hypothesis of the Anagrams. The Freud of the death drive must be pitted against the entire earlier edifice of psychoanalysis, and even against the Freudian version of the death drive" (*Echange*, p. 8). Death itself is for Baudrillard the ultimate symbol and therefore has to be reintegrated into our perception of reality in order to erase the Imaginary disjunction of life and death: "All of our culture is but an immense effort to dissociate life from death, to avert the ambivalence of death for the single benefit of reproducing life as value and time as its general equivalent. The repudiation of death is that phantasm of ours that extends its ramifications in all directions: it is the phantasm of life after death and of eternity for religions, it is the phantasm of truth for science, it is the phantasm of productivity and accumulation for the economy" (*Echange*, p. 225). This reabsorption of death in our culture will in turn subvert the Imaginary by introducing reversibility in all our discursive practices, by reinstating the Symbolic power of language. As a result, the Symbolic would put an end to "the linearity of time, to that of language, to that of economic exchanges and of accumulation, to that of power" (*Echange*, p. 8).

Clearly, Baudrillard's intention to discredit Foucault is directly related to the concerns outlined above: it has to be viewed in terms of a strategy aimed at the imperialism of discourses that support the Imaginary and that consolidate phantasms. Such, for example, are the theoretical constructs of Freud and Marx in Baudrillard's estimation: their systems are fundamentally tautological because their claim to truth is founded on an excision made in the Symbolic field, on a carefully selected area that has subsequently been privileged with an original and originating status—as primary process or as mode of production. Subjects, however, are nothing but discursive constructs and just as there never has been a linguistic subject, "there has never been an *economic subject, a homo oeconomicus*: this fiction has never been inscribed anywhere but in a code. Likewise, there has never been a *subject of consciousness,* and likewise there has never been a *subject of unconsciousness*" (*Echange,* p. 321). In the case of Foucault, Baudrillard points out that "the coherence and transparency of *homo sexualis* has never had more reality than that of *homo oeconomicus*" (*Oublier,* p. 40). Foucault is therefore to be seen as a generator of signs engaged in an impressive but futile codifying strategy that fits into a particular political economy of signs. He must be perceived as a mystifier because "there is mystification from the moment when there is rationalization in the name of whatever instance it might be. When the sexual is sublimated and rationalized in the political, social, or moral—but just as well when the Symbolic is censured and sublimated in a dominating sexual discourse" (*Echange,* p. 186). Foucault's discourse, thus supported by a "metaphysics of rationality," is bound to a fetishism of the signified, to a fascination with objects such as power and sexuality, objects that are nothing more than simulacra: "If it is at last possible to speak of power, of sexuality, of the body, of discipline, with this definitive intelligence, and about their slightest metamorphoses, it is because, somewhere, all this is already over and done with" (*Oublier,* p. 12). It means that we have completed another cycle in the epistemological spiral of Western thought and that the discourse which constitutes the present loop does nothing more than reflect the one below. In the final analysis, Foucault's discourse is a mirror of the process he describes and provides an account of its own teleonomical power with which it has replaced the theological and the teleological varieties. Foucault is not only fascinated by a "decoy of power" [*le leurre du pouvoir*], but has been caught by it, since he "unmasks all the final or causal illusions pertaining to power, but tells us nothing about *the simulacrum of power itself*" (*Oublier*, p. 55).

Far from effecting a break with established epistemological modes, Foucault's discourse thus provides a propitious alibi for the traditional systems of power operative in the West. Baudrillard finds that Foucault's treatment of power and sexuality only produces new simulacra that lend further support to the signifying practices of a society that exerts its domination with signs, "just as political economy and production realize their full scope only with the sanction and the blessing of Marx" (*Oublier*, pp. 35–36). Furthermore, though they may appear to contradict traditional interpretations, Foucault's writings really serve to animate and reanimate referents that are on the way out, visibly disintegrating all around us—that are, in a word, *révolus*. Only in this sense is Foucault's discourse revolutionary: it marks the end of a cycle and therefore manifests itself as a paroxysm because "the immanent death of all the great referentials (religious, sexual, political, etc.) manifests itself as an exacerbation of the forms of violence and of representation which characterized them" (*Oublier*, p. 84). The intense nature of Foucault's prose may give it an appearance of originality, but in the spiral of epistemological evolution his discourse is only a reflection, a representation of the cycle that is ending; it is a simulacrum empty of content, a form pretending to be content. The power of Foucault's writing is thus attributable to the fascination his discourse elicits, to the seduction it practices on the reader.

From Baudrillard's standpoint, however, the seduction of Foucault's discourse is incomplete for it does not reveal itself as such. Foucault does not go far enough in his analysis of power and of sexuality, and instead of contributing to the disintegration of these referents, he hypostatizes them. Having been caught by the lure of power and of sexuality, Foucault's discourse partakes of a general strategy of sense-production and is therefore subject to the disintegration that menaces all systems saturated with meaning: "*Any meaningful discourse wishes to put an end to appearances,* that is its lure and its imposture. But also an impossible enterprise: inexorably, discourse has to surrender to its own appearance, and thus to the game of seduction, and thus to *its own failure as a discourse*" (*Séduction,* p. 78). Discourse fascinates by its appearance, and its surface effects have an inevitable tendency to absorb its sense. Only the discourse of Lacan—"the Great Impostor"—has been successful in evading the lures of meaning and in realizing a consistently implosive strategy: Lacanian texts evolve in a hallucinated play of signifiers, which, in spite of their intention to erect a new Law, help to demolish the edifice of psychoanalysis, and "the most beautiful edifice of meaning and interpretation to have been erected crumbles thus under the weight and under the play of its own signs which, no longer heavy with meaning, have become the artifacts of an unbridled seduction, the unbridled terms of a collusive and meaningless exchange" (*Séduction,* p. 84). Lacan's discourse is the epitome of a general cultural process through which Reason, Sense, Law, are all disintegrating and giving way to Games, Exchange, and Ritual. This does not mean that all sense is being eliminated: only that it is no longer restricted to definite chains of coherence and that "any sign is vulnerable to other signs, that any sign can be seduced by other signs" (*Séduction,* p. 197).

In his two most recent publications, *De la séduction* and *Simulacres et simulation,* Baudrillard presents seduction as the ultimate remedy for the disenchantment brought about by a civilization that rests on nothing more than simulation and simulacra (this process of seduction is to be distinguished, however, from what Baudrillard identifies as the "cold seduction" of objects and of those social processes that operate according to norms and models, that is, the processes associated with the world of advertising and the promotion of conspicuous consumption). Modern society depends upon a strategy of simulation, on the production of simulacra—that is, of certain effects of truth intended to hide the fact that truth does not exist. It is therefore of no use to oppose new truths to existing ones or to reveal a new reality: the only effective way of coping with the insidiousness of social processes is to accept the Game for what it is: a Symbolic ritual. Everything—truth, power, being—is made reversible by the play of seduction, by the strategy of displacement (*se-ducere*) which puts an end to the production of reality and of truth: "Seduction is that which cannot possibly be represented, because the distance between the Real and its double, the distortion between the Same and the Other is abolished in it" (*Séduction*, p. 95). Seduction is a superficial, frivolous, and arbitrary process that recognizes no end, no purpose, no sense other than that of its own play.

We are to give ourselves up to this play of seduction in order to outwit the relentless conditioning imposed by a post-modern culture, in order to restore to our lives the meaningless sense of the Symbolic, in order to accentuate interhuman relations, because "we have been confusing obligation in its strong, ritual, immemorial sense—which it has in the cycle of men and things—with the trivialized constraint of the laws and codes that rule us under the opposite sign of liberty" (*Séduction*, p. 203). True freedom comes from the realization that there is nothing behind the proliferation of signs produced by post-modern culture. We must, according to Baudrillard, become aware of the simulation on which our civilization is predicated. Western capitalism has done away with values and referents, instead setting up exchange as regulatory mechanism and fundamental law. It is therefore thoroughly amoral and meaningless; at the same time, it seeks at all costs to preserve a facade of morality and meaning. That is why it needs crises, it needs to be attacked —in the name of reason and morality—so that "its instantaneous cruelty, its incomprehensible ferocity, its fundamental immorality" remain forever concealed (*Simulacres*, p. 29). Scandals, such as Watergate, are useful to hide the inherent scandalousness of the entire system. They are a part of an overall strategy designed to produce reality—to persuade everyone of the reality of moral and social referentials, of the seriousness of economic and political rationales.

The university is of course very much implicated in the production of simulacra and, while it is useful as an organ of custody and surveillance for a certain age group, its role is also to ensure the generation and the circulation of diplomas —to function as if there existed real values to support, actual principles to realize through this activity. But this referential dimension of academic endeavors is gradually dissipating, it is an "already dead and putrefying referential," and it is becoming obvious that "the exchange of signs (of knowledge, of culture) at the University, between those 'teaching' and those 'taught' has already been, for some time, nothing more than a collusion accompanied by the bitterness of indifference" (*Simulacres*, pp. 217, 224). Universities, together with all the other systems still striving to produce meaning, have become cancerous organisms saturating the social dimension with a senseless, relentless, and malignant proliferation of signs. Although this frenzied production of simulacra follows ever newer and more fashionable models such as the microscopic operation of genetic codes or the minute technology of electrons and although it is made highly efficient by the relentless and massive operation of information and communication networks, it is an activity rendered futile by its very prolixity. Like the process of information, which, "instead of producing sense . . . exhausts itself in the staging of sense," such a delirious and generalized process of simulation ends up by devouring its own contents.

In the implacable light of Baudrillard's revelations, we are left with little more than a melancholy fascination with the two-dimensional world of simulation, with the realization that "the only thing true, the only thing truly seductive is that which performs with one dimension less" (*Simulacres*,

p. 161). All fabrications of sense are illusory and futile while "appearances, they are immortal, invulnerable to even the nihilism of sense or of nonsense" (p. 236). Since this ultimate truth of our civilized existence cannot be transcended, "only a pataphysics of simulacra can free us from the system's strategy of simulation and of the deadly impasse in which it encloses us" (p. 222). Our lucidity will therefore require that we play along with the system by parodying it, by reproducing its mechanisms while revealing the factitiousness and artfulness of the game. In the university, this strategy will highlight the contrived status of the educator and the complicity of the student, but it will also make it necessary to grant the professor "if only a pinch of legitimacy taken from the ultra-left," thus making him into at least a "mannequin of power and of knowledge." In this guise, Baudrillard assures us, things can go on indefinitely, "because there is an end to value and to work, but there is none to the simulacrum of value and of work" (*Simulacres,* p. 226).

Baudrillard's discourse reaches thus a rather curious impasse. It has, so to speak, painted itself into a corner— with regard both to its critical intent and to its philosophical consistency. We must note, however, that it is a dilemma that Baudrillard himself clearly recognizes. Thus, while he clearly sympathizes with the critical thought of a radical left, with what he terms a "system of moral and economic equivalency," he also sees that the left is inevitably doomed to failure in its attempt to resurrect all the familiar referents of a bourgeois culture, to resuscitate "all the mechanisms of capitalism in order to be able to take them over one day" (*Simulacres,* p. 216). All these referents, as we have seen, are in a state of disintegration and, from Baudrillard's standpoint, a critical enterprise should only try to speed up this process. Offering the "putrefaction" of the university as an example, he suggests transforming "this rotting into a violent process, into a violent death, by means of derision, defiance, and a multiplied simulation that would offer the ritual death of the University as the model of putrefaction for the whole of society, as a contagious model of disaffection for an entire social structure, in which death would finally wreak its havoc" (*Simulacres*, p. 217). Baudrillard considers himself to be a "terrorist and a nihilist in theory just as others are with weapons" recognizing that "theoretical violence, and not truth, is the only resource we have left" (p. 235). Although he also realizes that even this attitude still makes sense, since it is predicated on a radicalness that is ultimately utopian in nature, he adopts it in preference to any other in the hope of furthering the general process of disintegration that will lead to a cataclysmic implosion of all systems of knowledge. Baudrillard's discourse thus ends up by invalidating all ontological and epistemological foundations for critical activity—producing instead the mirror of its own superior vision as its justification.

Indeed, it is a discourse that seduces itself by foreclosing the reality of everything outside its own Imaginary boundaries. Intent on situating itself above all other critical strategies, it puts itself forward as a higher aesthetics. Yet, in the end, Baudrillard is able only to offer the intellectually refined pleasure of seduction and the sterile satisfaction of a lucidity that precludes all meaningful action. In this regard, his discourse culminates in a strikingly Nietzschean posture and adopts the sort of course that Jean Starobinski has identified as a characteristic of certain modern denunciations of illusion: "This course consists of conferring, by an act of *my* will, a higher value on that system of values of which *I* am the source, and to which no transcendent absolute can be opposed. Against a background of nothingness, power and force thus compel recognition as the sole appearance that is not illusion. This aesthetic option veers into a sort of activism: it chooses action for the sake of action, instead of abiding by the choice of convention for the sake of convention."[28] It is clear that Baudrillard's discourse displays a

28. Jean Starobinski, "Montaigne on Illusion: The Denunciation of Untruth," *Daedalus*, 108 (1977), 98.

radicalness lacking in that of the more "conventional" Foucault, whose work exploits the Symbolic ties that bind the
human community. Foucault's (perhaps illusory) search for
new conventions, carried out while he dismantles the established modes of subjection, brings with it the force of a
concern for that frustrated and alienated part of humanity
still struggling to live and to find some sense for itself. Having demystified this civilization, Baudrillard savors the supreme hopelessness of his vision. Still exploring, Foucault
assumes the risks involved in the production of new meanings and, at the same time, strives to maintain his discourse
open, attentive, and receptive to the unknown potential of
the Symbolic.

To put it simply, the discourse of Foucault is devoid of the
pretentiousness of Baudrillard's critique. Baudrillard claims
for his work the status of metaphor: it is presented as an accurate illustration of the fundamental characteristics of Western civilization, as the simulacrum of modern culture and its
strategies of simulation. In addition, by positing the hyperreality of simulacra as a reality that cannot be transcended,
Baudrillard's writing ends up by capitulating to the rule
of the Imaginary. It reaches an intellectual impasse, a position that recognizes nothing beyond a play of mirrors destined endlessly to reflect signs and images that can have
no meaning beyond the infinitely regressive semiosis of the
disembodied language in which they are trapped. Baudrillard
reaches this impasse because he pursues the arguments deriving from his basic premises to their bitter, logical end. It is
a procedure that Foucault rejects—although it is clear that,
in certain respects, his writing is predicated on premises
similar to those underlying Baudrillard's project: thus, in
commenting on the achievement of Nietzsche, Foucault says
that "interpretation can never be brought to an end simply
because there is nothing to interpret. There is nothing absolutely primary to be interpreted, since fundamentally, everything is already interpretation; every sign is, in itself, not the
thing susceptible to interpretation but the interpretation of

other signs."[29] Foucault does not, however, make such insights into critical dogma, nor does he develop them into the logic of systems, into instruments of the Same. For Foucault, language remains the locus of the Other; it is connected to bodies and is contiguous with their desires but its attempts to transcribe these are vain: language, as well as the systems it builds, can be only an inadequate means of representing our existence. It is in this sense that the discourse of Michel Foucault can be recognized as an effective critique of the Same: Foucault resists its entrapment by orienting his writing toward the insuperable proximity of the Other, by referring it to the endless possibilities the Symbolic provides for transgressing the limitations of established meanings.[30]

29. Foucault, "Nietzsche, Freud, Marx," *Cahiers du Royaumont: Nietzsche* (Paris: Minuit, 1967), p. 189.

30. Although my purpose has not been to examine the critical reactions to the thought of Michel Foucault in the United States, I should note that the basic concerns relating to the issue of identity versus difference are to be found in the analyses of American critics as well. There is, for example, the issue of *Humanities in Society* (Winter 1980) devoted to a discussion of Foucault's impact on the study of the humanities. One particular theme broached by some of the articles relates to the "uses and abuses" of Foucault: it reflects a concern that Foucault's work not turn into yet another academic discipline and thereby lose its validity as a radical critique (see, for example, the articles by Michael Sprinker and by Paul Bové). When discussed in the context of a critical usefulness, Foucault has been frequently contrasted with Derrida in American criticism. Comparisons linking Foucault to Derrida are inevitable because of certain similarities of purpose but also because Foucault and Derrida represent the two most significant recent French intellectual imports into this country. Among the articles that raise the issue of the critical merit of archaeology and deconstruction, I have found the following particularly cogent: Edward W. Said, "The Problem of Textuality: Two Exemplary Positions," *Critical Inquiry* 4, no. 4 (Summer 1978); Said, "Reflections on Recent American 'Left' Literary Criticism," *Boundary 2* 8, no. 1 (Fall 1979); Joseph N. Riddel, "Re-Doubling the Commentary," *Contemporary Literature 20*, no. 2 (Spring 1979); Dominick LaCapra, "Rethinking Intellectual History and Reading Texts," *History and Theory* 19, no. 3 (1980); William V. Spanos, "Retrieving Heidegger's De-Struction," *SCE Reports*, no. 8 (Fall 1980); E. M. Henning, "Foucault and Derrida: Archaeology and Deconstruction," *Stanford French Review* 2 (Fall 1981); and Alexander Argyros, "The Possibility of History," *New Orleans Review* 8, no. 3 (Fall 1981).

Conclusion

Although subversive, Foucault's critical undertaking is not characterized by aimless theoretical terrorism; it accepts its ties with its own cultural archive as inevitable but it also uses these connections for its own critical purposes. Foucault's archaeology accomplishes this, as we have seen, through a process of inversion, of tactical reversals and, in a more general sense, by means of a metonymical conjunction with existing modes of exegesis and interpretation—a procedure it employs without assimilating the strategies of the more conventional approaches. In order not to reproduce metaphorically the principal element of an anthropological discursive practice, Foucault replaces some basic themes of intellectual activity with their contiguous counterparts: discourse as plenitude with discourse as practice, depth with surface, meaning with event, reason with unreason, legality with illegality, presence with absence, knowledge as revelation with knowledge as power, the sciences of life and of reason with the void of death and the delirium of madness, the subject as being with the subject as an outline in a discursive configuration, in short, as I have argued, the Imaginary with the Symbolic. As with all metonymical relationships, however, this process of substitution does not work to eliminate the first term of the enumerated pairings: it keeps it in mind while producing a new conceptualization made possible by the second term. By operating in conjunction with the trace of the first term, the second term of the metonymical association provides us with a perspective on a third component—the Real, that is, the reality of the subject as it is constituted at the conjunction of the Imaginary and the Symbolic.

Initially, of course, Foucault's writings can suggest a negative, anarchistic purpose and, as we have seen, this alleged nihilism has been a common theme in some of the polemical debate surrounding his books. Ultimately, however, it seems indisputable that Foucault's enterprise is eminently positive—simply because it is, in its critical thrust, the negation of a negation: it highlights what has asserted itself as a positive force in Western culture—that is, those areas of knowledge inspired by a positivistic outlook—and presents it as a systematic negation and exclusion. What has been negated, from Foucault's perspective, is that dimension of the human experience which is not amenable to conscious and rational control. It might well be argued that, if such is the case, Foucault's project does nothing more than refurbish an ancient and familiar archetype of man and that his discourse simply produces its own version of our humanity. Yet, even if it were possible to reconstruct a particular model of human nature from Foucault's writings, this would not invalidate his enterprise—first, because it is probably impossible to develop any critical strategy without implying some vision of the nature of our humanity and, second, because this issue is really unimportant from the perspective of archaeology's effect. Foucault's explicit purpose, what he conceives to be the most pressing need, is the liberation of man from the images that have contributed to subjugate him in the name of various ideals and interests.

Perhaps the most obvious indication of an implicit, a priori notion of a human nature is provided by Foucault's attitude toward the notion and the function of the intellect. It is a position that appears close to that of Antonio Gramsci, for whom intellectualism was a fundamentally human trait, a birthright peculiar to the human species. Foucault, we have seen, discredits the professional "universal intellectual" who aspires to the status of guru and who claims the prerogative of telling others how and for what purposes to live. However, although Foucault grants everyone the intellectual privilege of determining the direction and goals of one's existence and struggles, he also appears to make this privilege conditional on the acquisition of a special awareness. It is what I have called an awareness of the Symbolic, of all that conditions and predisposes our ways of knowing and speaking. It is also an awareness of the need to think genealogically, that is, relentlessly to reexamine our historical antecedents, to review the story of all that has brought us to our present modes of conceptualization. Yet it seems doubtful that such a genealogical vocation can develop without the benefit of a pedagogical process, and here once more the strategy of Foucault's critique manifests its predilection for paradox: it makes the intellect into an attribute of the common man, it supports what he has called the "struggles against the privileges of knowledge," but by its own example, it shows this critique to be effective only when involved in the rigorous and demanding life of the disciplines of knowledge, only when it realizes itself as a "relentless erudition."

As a critique of intellectual activity, Foucault's discourse is obviously aimed at "intellectuals": it selects, by its very constitution, those minds trained to think in appropriately subtle and complicated ways. But this particular function of Foucault's discourse also entails the greatest potential for critical effectiveness. By demonstrating that our knowledge of truth derives from a selective and reductive process that implicitly assumes the unknown to be irrelevant, by indicting all the self-sufficient procedures that delimit our nature only to be in a better position to control us, Foucault's approach realizes its greatest potential in counteracting those highly selective intellectual strategies that have given rise to rationales of subjection and have made the tyranny of intellect possible.

Index

Index

Index

Sexuality, 104–106; as knowledge-power, 112–113; politics of, 110–112; as simulacrum, 156–157. *See also* Power-truth; Truth
Sheridan, Alan, 121, 147
Signified, 35, 153
Signifier, 18–19, 34–36, 153
Simulacra and simulation, 150, 152, 158–160, 163
Simulacres et simulation, 158
Social sciences. *See* Human sciences
Spanos, William V., 164
Sprinker, Michael, 164
Starobinski, Jean, 162
Subject, 16, 18–19, 30–37, 73, 79; and anthropology, 29, 64; in Baudrillard, 156; Foucault as, 39, 133; as function, 137; as historical product of discourse, 80; and meaning, 33; and normalization, 105–106; as product of power, 110. *See also* Discourse; Imaginary; Language; Signifier; Symbolic
Subjection, 16, 27, 100, 133. *See also* Domination
Subversion, 17, 78, 82, 141. *See also* Inversion
Symbolic, 19, 30–37; in Baudrillard, 154–156, 159; and discursive relations, 87; and madness, 42–51; mediation of, in Foucault, 131–132,

136; as morality, 137; and outside of discourse, 116; and power-knowledge, 111; and reality, 41; and religion, 43; as transgression, 164. *See also* Archaeology; *énoncé*; *episteme*; Imaginary; Real

Theory, 123–125; function of, 127–130. *See also* Intellectual
Truth, 34, 38, 128, 137; as alienation, 47; of man, 30, 103; political nature of, 20, 104–106, 125; will to, 28. *See also* Anthropocentrism; Imaginary; Knowledge; Normalization; Power-knowledge; Sexuality
Tuke, Samuel, 47

Unconscious, 34, 38; sciences of, 41. *See also* Symbolic
University, 160–162
Unreason, 21, 45–49; and confinement, 46–47. *See also* Madness

Van Gogh, Vincent, 49
Veyne, Paul, 76

Wahl, François, 83
Watergate, 160
White, Hayden, 18
Wilden, Anthony, 36

Michel Foucault and the
Subversion of Intellect

Designed by Richard E. Rosenbaum.
Composed by Eastern Graphics
in 10 point Linotron 202 Palatino, 3 points leaded,
with display lines in Palatino.
Printed offset by Braun-Brumfield, Inc. on
Warren's Number 66 Antique Offset, 50 pound basis.
Bound by John H. Dekker & Sons, Inc.
in Joanna book cloth
and stamped in Kurz-Hastings foils.

Library of Congress Cataloging in Publication Data

Racevskis, Karlis.
Michel Foucault and the subversion of intellect.

Includes index.
1. Foucault, Michel. I. Title.
B2430.F724R33   1983   194   82-22090
ISBN 0-8014-1572-1